THE BOOK OF JOSHUA

Praise for *The Book of Joshua*

'This book is a must-have … an enduring tale of finding love and its meaning'—*Sunday Guardian*

'A compelling read—you will remember this dog for all time'—*Sunday Mid-day*

'A joyous romp'—*Hindu*

'*The Book of Joshua* will warm your heart'—*Asian Age*

'This passionate tribute is like no other'—Dogs and More

'Mendonsa's mirth is infectious'—*Mail Today*

'I read *The Book of Joshua* from cover to cover and by the end of it I was crying … it's fantastic'—*Telegraph*

'A must read … charming'—Pritish Nandy

THE BOOK OF JOSHUA

the true story of a dog who loved the world

tanya mendonsa

HarperCollins *Publishers* India

First published in 2012 by
HarperCollins *Publishers* India
A–75, Sector 57, Noida, Uttar Pradesh 201301, India
www.harpercollins.co.in

This edition published in 2020

2 4 6 8 10 9 7 5 3 1

P-ISBN: 978-93-5029-137-5
E-ISBN: 978-93-5029-550-2

Typeset in 11/14 Joanna MT Std at
Manipal Technology Ltd, Manipal

Printed and bound at
Thomson Press (India) Ltd

FSC MIX Paper FSC™ C010615

This book is produced from independently certified FSC™ paper to ensure responsible forest management.

For all the dog-lovers of the world—especially Antonio and Mallika—and for Joshua, who made us better than we were before

'I am I, because my little dog knows me'

—Gertrude Stein

Lay Your Head, Darling, Darling, Darling

Lay your head, darling, darling, darling
Your darling black head my heart above.
O mouth of honey with the thyme for fragrance,
Who with heart in his breast could deny you love?
(anonymous Irish ballad)

And what shall I do when that beloved weight is removed?
Removed by accident, or old age, or some other, deadly, mortal worm?

When the total trust of flinging one body upon another - in such sure knowledge that that other body will be there - is absent from my daily and nightly sleep?

And what can replace that dual vision,
when we sit in silence in the dusk and look upon the world?

In silence, he wraps his paw around my forearm,
and I lean my head upon his cheek.
I breathe in his breath,
as comforting as warm bread on a cold morning.

We both laugh with joy at nothing: just happy to be alive.
Who will laugh with me, in perfect unison, when two becomes one?

If I gave you half my lifespan, we could go out together:

close our eyes and leap the chasm together,

into that other world

where two into one

is one forevermore.

In the Beginning There Was the Cocker Spaniel

WHEN I FINALLY SAT DOWN ONE EVENING TO WRITE THE STORY OF Joshua my first thought was that I needed to find a publisher abroad because Joshua doesn't have too many fans in India—too many fans who know him, that is. However, those whom he has never met, at home or abroad, find him a never-ending source of fascination. This fascination has less to do with what he actually does and more with the effect he has on us.

Of course, a cocker spaniel is a cocker spaniel the world over. Anybody who has once fallen under the spell of those anguished eyes gazing into yours, declaring that you are the Master of their Universe, that silky paw pushing insistently at your cheek at 3 a.m. when he wants to go out, that rollicking bark straight from the belly as he rolls on the grass after a meal, that velvety muzzle ... but let me not get carried away (or not just yet, although in the opinion of many of those dear friends who are not fans of Josh I should have been sent to take a 'rest' in some secluded place, several times a year, preferably taking him along).

Joshua is old and grey, going on fifteen at the time of writing this book, but he was far from being full of sleep.

He may not have been able to run the way he did as a pup, with all four legs simultaneously off the ground, like a spring lamb, but he insisted on a walk every couple of hours. Unfortunately for us, even at night. Blind as he was, he had figured that it made no difference. We lived (and still do) in the mountains where there are panthers, bears and bison at large after dusk, so he had to be taken out on a leash. It may be romantic to see the stars blazing in the milky way at midnight, or the full moon sinking into the valley at 3 a.m., but we felt like hell the next morning. Naturally, Joshua had a prolonged lie-in, in his new bed, with his new quilts, recovering from the adventures of the night, while we staggered on with the business of a new day.

Of course, slower on his feet and medicated for his heart, he was watched anxiously by Antonio and myself every time he had a coughing fit, yet he still attacked his meals with the starving concentration of someone shipwrecked for a week, and adored parties more than ever. There was none of the usual mood of warming both hands at the fire of life, believing that 'it sinks and I am ready to depart' in Joshua's take on ageing.

The fire of life was still inside him, and he kept it blazing merrily for as long as he possibly could.

Naturally, I felt like I couldn't ever leave him. I recently went away for a fortnight for urgent family reasons, but apparently Joshua terrified everyone by not eating, not sleeping, and padding around in search of me until he was breathless. A friend came to stay and help; the long journey to the vet, made over the mountain roads was in desperation, but the instant I came back the patient made a miraculous recovery. Leaping like a young gazelle, he rejoiced; he ate like a boa constrictor, he rejoiced again. Finally, he fell into a deep, untroubled and abandoned sleep in his favourite posture; on his back with a paw braced against me, and didn't budge for over twelve hours. His love was home, and all was well with the world once more. Of course, I had to stay in bed too—that goes without saying—for fear of waking him.

The first thing I would feel again, each and every morning would be a big, icy cold nose touching mine, greeting me to a new day, packed with enjoyment.

From the time I was little, I identified people by the dogs they had. Fortunately, growing up in the Calcutta of the 1960's, I had many four-legged friends that came with their two-legged attachments. But, in our family, we had always had cocker spaniels. Cocker spaniels of every colour and variety … sometimes with a dash of mongrel, sometimes without: coal-black, blue-roan, spangled-blonde, speckled-rust, deep-tawny. All boys.

But Joshua was a revelation to me. Not only did he come into my life at a vital moment, but he was also—luckily for both of us, as all of us know how dangerous unfulfilled expectations can be—my soulmate in every way.

When I was twenty-one, I left Calcutta for Paris, where I would spend the following twenty years. The idea of Love and the Ideal Husband were as firmly intertwined in my head as I hoped I'd myself be, someday, in that man's arms.

Eighteen years on, nothing had changed except for the second part of the equation: for Husband, substitute Dog.

But in that interim, my life had undergone many, many sea changes before I'd had my epiphany.

The best time to make dramatic changes is when there's nothing dramatic going on. My little universe was ticking over nicely (apart from a heart that weighed more than I did at that point, over a prolonged bout of unrequited love). But, during one of my annual rejuvenating trips back to Goa to visit my family, I suddenly realised there was something missing: I wasn't as happy to go back to Paris that January as I generally was.

Back in my flat, for about the first time in my life, I sat down on the floor of my hallway, stone-cold sober, and emptied my mind slowly of all practicalities—job, business partner, employees, friends, lovers, lame ducks—until I had created a great, big, empty space to think in. I took a deep breath and asked my gut what it wanted, and it instantly shouted back—

'A dog! I want that cocker spaniel, that little black and white boy—I can almost smell that milky breath, I feel that ice-cold nose, I'm kissing that silky head, I want him, I want him, I want him *now*!'

'What else?' I asked my gut.

'A garden,' it replied, not shouting any longer, but crooning seductively, 'a garden to write and to paint in.'

'That's it?'

'That's it.'

I then rapidly calculated in my head how long it would actually take me to get things in order to be able to change continents with a clear conscience; I arrived at the figure of two years, wrote down the corresponding date, put on Leonard Cohen ('*Songs of Love and Hate*', an all-time favourite, some things don't change), and already romping in that mythical garden with my mythical pup, proceeded to get happily drunk.

I never regretted that decision. For a while, nobody really took me very seriously. Of course, my business partner buried his head in the sand and would listen to no talk of training a replacement for me. It was only when I finally packed up my desk and told him it was my last day on the job (having already written myself a severance cheque and paid my taxes in advance), showing him my one-way ticket from Paris to Bangalore that he started like a bolting horse and began to charge around—opening file cabinets and rummaging around in them as if he hoped to find the Rosetta stone. But my mind was made up. The subsequent slide of the business into bankruptcy (although I had built it so carefully) is a story that deviates from its main objective, who at that point was barely a gleam in his father's eye, as my own father would have said.

It was only when I started packing up my flat that all the comrades started wailing, 'But why now?'

'When, then?' was all I could reply.

Always better to leave at a high point in one's life (except for the still-aching heart, but that is a given when one is a woman—a given, that is, until you find your dog) when no reason, except something primeval deep inside you tells you it's time to go. Never wait until some negative event pushes you to leave, especially onto what you have persuaded yourself will be a wonderful new road, but which only turns out to be either a dead-end or a loop back to the beginning.

My business partner, an Englishman who knew even less about 'business' than I, and was still living in the days of Disraeli in his mind, had been in the habit of buying rather extravagant birthday presents for me (eighteenth century miniatures painted on ivory, which I put into the washing machine;

tiny antique silver stamp cases, that disappeared forever into the torn lining of my shoulder bag; Victorian rings, left on someone else's windowsills and so on). One year, we were in Kent, and happened to pass a junk shop. And I saw his image in the window: the head of a blue-roan cocker spaniel, with all the best and beautiful attributes of the breed, painted upon a dessert plate. 'That's what I want for my birthday!' I shouted, clutching his arm. 'But it costs 25 pence!' he replied, outraged. 'I don't care how cheap it is, I want it!'

Twenty-five-years later (and I lost many, many gifts in the interval, but never that plate), when Joshua was about two years old, you could hold the plate next to his face and not find any difference—he is the image of the image—come and see for yourself if I'm exaggerating!

Having bid a tearful farewell to all the comrades (including a riotous leaving party at Charles de Gaulle airport), and armed with the very best book on cocker spaniels available in Paris at WH Smith on the Rue de Rivoli, lavishly illustrated and gripping enough to illuminate a twelve-hour journey, I flew back to India in search of the beloved.

At 3 a.m. on a Tuesday morning at Mumbai airport in 1995 (after a blissful flight spent reciting poetry with the Air India steward all night), I was groggily collecting a trolley for my luggage when an overweight, middle-aged man hit me in the ribs with his elbow and grabbed the trolley from me.

Did the event dent my euphoria?

Nah.

I hadn't come back to India to find a man; I'd come back for a dog to find me.

And as a smug Jane Eyre says at the end of the novel, 'Reader, I married him.' His name is not Rochester but Joshua, and he lives simply for pleasure. As we have the perfect union, I have adopted his way of life and without the slightest trace of guilt.

I won't start producing nude baby photos at this point, but will only say he was the most beautiful boy in the world, and even when he was old by dog standards (and blind, like Rochester, but so much nicer), the years only added to his perfection. 'If I can't have too many truffles,' said Colette (who also said that our perfect companions are all four-legged), 'I'll do without.'

That is Joshua's and my joint philosophy too, but metaphorically speaking, we generally see to it that we have too many truffles.

We find each other the funniest, truest, best and most absorbing beings in the whole world. What better foundation for the good life can there be, more than that of unquestioning mutual adoration?

We both like the same things and the same people. We never argue. We howl when we're sad and laugh when we're happy. Our two hearts beat as one. He leads me when we walk together, but, then, there is his masculine ego for me to cherish.

Of course, we have our faults—the worst being an indelible streak of stubbornness. Once an idea is firmly planted in our heads, it's practically impossible to uproot it, impossible unless we have a bout of amnesia. Drag Josh away from a certain spot he's determined to investigate and the very next time he's out on a walk, he'll rush unerringly towards it and insist on raking over every scrap of evidence. When he's finally done—and nothing can hurry him up—he pees copiously all over the exact spot before covering it with a contemptuous shower of earth, back legs working furiously. Moreover, we forgive, but we never forget; once bitten, twice shy, and there's no point in talking about turning the other cheek. Although we're both renegades, we're also creatures of routine and tend to be overly trusting. We love unwisely and too well. For the rest, we pretty much take life as we find it, and we generally find it to be luscious.

It is an indisputable fact that dog lovers tend to be nice people—open, generous, creative and unconventional (and dog lovers know best). Our unkinder critics would label these qualities respectively 'foolishly trusting', 'spendthrift', 'lazy' and 'not quite all there'. But they know nothing of the joy of being so ecstatically greeted—even after an absence of five minutes—they see only the muddy paw marks on our white shirts. At cocktail time, they don't remark on the amazing athletic ability of our darlings indoors— they're just too busy picking cucumber dip out of their hair. You would think that anyone with a grain of sense would recognize their astonishing luck at having Joshua (so handsome, so urbane, such a gifted conversationalist!) as a dinner partner—but no, they're looking at their plate wiped clean before they've eaten a single bite.

But all these killjoys are forgotten in the company of one's fellow enthusiasts. These are the *real* people, with *real* values. With four-legged bodies cosily surrounding us (sometimes on top of us) and plenty of good food and good drink to be communally shared (Josh is especially partial to a good calvados), we swap stories of our canine partners.

Their astonishing intelligence ('You see, he has such an eye for people: he bit the electrician and they just found out he's dealing drugs—well, he's safe in the hospital now'); their latest fads ('It's really lovely to have to get up to walk at

2 a.m.—you discover a whole new world!'); their culinary preferences (the first cake I ever baked was for Josh; I'm at the ciabatta with black olives stage now, and he's so proud of me). There are hot debates on medication (this, of course, involves riveting stories of midnight anguish, last minute crises and miraculous recoveries).

I do actually have a two-legged male—a great artist called Antonio E Costa—in my life now, but I have to admit that the reason he is still in it is because he immediately, wisely and from the very beginning, ceded first place to Joshua, thus letting the best man win and ensuring harmony in the home. Secondly, he's almost as mad about the boy as I am, which makes for positively good music!

One piece of advice: listen to your gut and let it lead you to your destined dog.

With that out of the way, we can get down to the nitty gritty: those nude baby photos.

Here's the one commemorating his first bark ... look at that face ... have you ever seen anything as marvellous as that look in his eyes? Is that adorable, or is that adorable?

Kiss me quick, Josh, before I swoon all over again.

In a way, our relationship was much like an old-fashioned arranged marriage: both parties involved come to the table hoping for love and willing to give it. Of course, it helps if both parties are also attractive. As a one-time artist and a hopeful poet, I was unashamedly drawn to beauty and, by gum, Joshua was the most beautiful baby I'd ever seen and he only became more so as he grew.

He was three weeks old when I first kissed him. He was velvety white and had almost perfect pure-black markings: the classic white blaze down the domed forehead and over the muzzle, black patches round his eyes all the way up to his ears the size of small postage stamps, and symmetrical black patches all the way down his back. His milky dark blue eyes were filmed with sleep, his tiny paws dangled like a chipmunk's; he snuffled gently into my palm and blew me into a new life.

Marking Time

BEFORE WE CONTINUE WITH THE BABY PICTURES, HOWEVER, WE HAVE to fill in the gaps by introducing the third party—the masculine two-legged part of the picture.

Antonio and I met roughly a year after I'd arrived back in India to live in Bangalore and start my lending library called 'Silver Moon'.

There was a party to celebrate the end of a workshop for international women artists, and I'd been invited by a literary friend to 'meet new people'. During the event, Antonio, who'd come down from Canada to organize the workshop ('give me women every time,' he's said to me on countless subsequent occasions, 'they're the only sex I can relate to') was the only new person I met, because, at first sight, we abandoned the throng and spent the rest of the evening together. 'How many years have you guys known each other?' asked the host. We didn't bother to reply—at the same moment, we'd spotted the resident dog chained up on the veranda—we moved as one to join him in the moonlight and share our dinner.

Later, Antonio said to me (and how I treasure this! How I wish he'd say it to me every day!), 'the first time I saw you, I saw the sun in your face.'

It was fate: we spent the rest of the evening feeding the dog our dinners, and I knew—the distance between Canada and India notwithstanding—I'd found the father of my future love.

In a matter of weeks, Antonio had to leave for Brazil for a six month residency; it would take quite a while before we linked our destinies and formed the eternal triangle. However, he called me every Sunday, and would hold the receiver away from himself and say, 'listen to the sea'. He also sent weekly letters full of incoherent plans for our future (this before we had no more than clasped hands), stuffed with pressed wild flowers.

In the meantime, I poured all my energy into making 'Silver Moon' a labour of love. I had reproduced my own library of books, added all the Indian authors, shelved a wall full of children's books, put rugs down on the floor, Mucha prints on up the walls and eagerly awaited those avid readers who mostly never arrived. I had saved up enough money to lose it for a purpose—nobody ever made any money from a bookstore. I had had more than enough of business while I was in France and was determined never again to have anything to do with it. A lending library seemed like the perfect idea. My little sister Sunita, who also lived in Bangalore with her young family at that point, gave me a calendar listing every known holiday in India and on each occasion I promptly closed the library. This led Deepak, one of my old friends from Calcutta (who had moved to the same city) to ask which day of the week I was actually open. He went on to explain that in India people *only* went to bookshops or libraries on holidays and if I wished to *see* any of the members of 'Silver Moon', let alone earn a little money, I would have to open a little oftener. And I did, but only because I was helped by a darling trio of sisters: Smita, Swati and Sneha Gowda, who were even prouder of the library than I was, but even sterner with borrowers who lived on an unvarying diet of Sidney Sheldon, Michael Crichton and the like.

The stage was almost set for the arrival of Joshua, but there was, as in the Bible, a forerunner by the name of Romeo, before the main attraction arrived in a blaze of glory. I had rented a beautiful little ground-floor flat in an area called Cooke Town, and I still think is the prettiest apartment I have ever lived in. It had a miniscule strip of garden along one side, which was no place to bring up a puppy, although I was very quickly adopted by a cat. This was a tabby tom; a rugged heavyweight with wary, pea-green eyes, a ginger topknot and a face crisscrossed by scars won in dishonourable battle. I had seen (and heard) these battles on the other side of my low garden wall and had often been rudely awakened in the small hours by a triumphant yell, signalling the defeat of yet another pretender to the role of *capo di tutti i capi* of the neighbourhood.

I had never had much truck with cats before, except for the fabled Bunny, the grey and neutered tom in Paris, who was the apple of my dearest friend Lavinia's eye. Bunny had often been left with me while Lav travelled, and I can't say that either of us was richer for the experience. In fact, if Bunny could have spoken, I doubt if Lav would have talked to me ever again. However, he lived to be twenty, which means that he couldn't have suffered too much from his experiences *chez moi*.

It was only when my mother Gilda, who was a brilliant cook and had written many cookbooks—*The Best of Goan Cooking* was already a classic—came to stay that Romeo (for so I had named him—I only found out much later that all the neighbours called him Saddam Hussein) crossed my garden wall and entered the house, ensnared by the intoxicating vapour from the kitchen that signalled fish curry, rich beef stew and prawn pickle. My mother, who loved all creatures—even crows—immediately swung into action, and the fishmonger (who came to the door) became a daily visitor.

Romeo was welcomed into my home with baby pomfrets (a delicate sea fish that is very expensive), lightly fried and served thrice a day on a fluffy bed of white rice. In between, he would drop in for bowls of milk, a snack of fruit cake or sardine sandwiches (cut into little squares by my mother to prevent choking).

After my mother went back to her home in Goa (leaving detailed instructions for the fish man), I was on my own. Having never cooked in my life I had to come to terms with even lighting the gas stove. See, all my friends in Paris were wonderful cooks; besides, back then, I used to go out for dinner practically every night.

Back in India, the microwave had become my god. With all the cheap and wonderful restaurants at every corner of the road in Cooke Town—nearly all of them happy to deliver even small orders—my culinary tasks were confined to moving pre-cooked packages of food from the freezer to the microwave.

In fact, my bosom friend from Bangalore, Arunesh (himself a superlative cook), later told me that at my parties he'd be puzzled by the sight of the empty kitchen and that, after asking people if they preferred vegetarian food or not, I would produce food for twenty people in ten minutes. Of course, it helped that the bar was always full and most people were too happily high to be fussy about what they were eating.

My ineptness in the kitchen was so well known that, when Antonio first met my mother in Goa, she immediately pressed him to carry a large plastic jar of prawn curry for me. The jar had a label on which she had written, in large letters, 'please decant, put in a saucepan and heat gently before serving'.

You get the picture!

Anyway, I did my best for Romeo as far as I could, without even attempting to reach the heights of my mother's culinary marvels. I finally bought him mackerels as they were cheaper and easier to deal with. I would split them, stuff them with my mother's famous spice mixture and fry them crisply on either side—which wasn't as easy as it sounds and which I finally managed to master after ruining at least a dozen frying pans and being marked with many painful burns all the way up to both elbows.

Romeo liked his meals freshly prepared, so the fish wasn't soggy or cold. Purposefully, he would land on my chest in the middle of the night, generally smelling like a can of garbage, and let loose a piercing series of yowls until I fell out of bed, grabbed the frying pan and did my stuff, with Ro lying on his back on the kitchen floor and screaming as if he'd been shot.

One Sunday, I had to meet some friends for lunch at Koshy's, one of the city's oldest and most loved restaurants. I was preparing to leave when Romeo—in one of his rare, loving moods—hooked his paws around my ankles and refused to let go. As I was already late, I scooped him up and dumped him in the green wicker basket I carried everywhere with me and set off. When we got there, Romeo was at his most urbane. The owner of Koshy's, Prem Koshy, was a famous animal lover, and on being told that Ro was an equally famous gourmand, at once took him on a tour of the kitchens. On his return, Romeo jumped on to the chair next to me, wrapped his tail around himself and sat up, ready for business.

'Let's see what they can rustle up round here,' his twitching nose said. Even before we had ordered, Prem bustled over with a plate of ladyfish fillets that he placed reverently on the table in front of Romeo. Romeo's eyes narrowed; he leaned forward cautiously and inhaled. He then sat back, snorted, and with a contemptuous flick of his paw, flipped all the fillets at one shot from the plate to the floor. Prem, instead of giving this ungrateful and uninvited guest a whack on the jaw, was heartbroken. Ever after, when I came to Koshy's, he would ask wistfully about Romeo and what he was eating that week!

Daddy's Home!

SINCE I HAD NO INTENTION OF LEAVING INDIA, ANTONIO, BY NOW in his mid-fifties, bravely turned his back on the existence as a wandering artist and threw in his lot with me.

I had no idea what to expect ... this was a man (admittedly like me, of Goan origin), born in Africa, who had left home as I had, at twenty-one, to study architecture and fine art in Canada, whose history sounded like a medieval jongleur's. In fact, the chief guest at one of his exhibitions in his introductory speech said that Antonio's life sounded like that of a travel agent on speed.

As a graduate student, he had managed to wangle a sabbatical to complete his thesis on architecture. He spent it on the island of Crete, where he was known as 'Adonis' and where he initially lived in a donkey stable. Well into his first year there, he was sitting hard at work one day, on a clifftop overlooking the crinkling blue sea. Presently, an elderly and sinewy goatherd friend called Yanni joined him on the grass.

Yanni unpacked his lunch of black olives, goat's cheese and bread and spread it out between them, having already uncorked a bottle of the local wine—'Dragon's Blood'.

As they drank and ate companionably, Yanni pointed to the drawings Antonio had been working on. 'Where are those buildings?' he asked.

'In Amrika,' replied Antonio. He had no desire to embark on explanations of Canada, especially since Yanni was illiterate.

'I don't understand,' said Yanni plaintively. 'You're sitting here in Crete, drinking this good wine, and wasting your time drawing pictures of buildings in Amrika?'

'Frankly, I don't understand either—it seems like a total waste of time,' said Antonio. He then ceremoniously wrapped up the thesis and together they threw it down to the sea far below, which swallowed it up without a murmur as they raised another glass to the end of an academic career.

After that, Antonio just painted. He travelled the world, wherever his fancy took him, from Crete to Mexico to Andalusia and other parts, picking up nine languages along the way and always travelling light.

When, over the protests of his long-time Canadian friends ('You hardly know this woman!') he turned to Bangalore, I went to meet him at the airport. There was a large roll of his paintings slung over his shoulder, and he was carrying two small bags, which held all he needed. One bag contained his worldly goods; the other was crammed with virgin olive oil, German knives, exotic peppercorns, Japanese seaweed and varied kitchen implements. It was clear that he'd come prepared to stay. He didn't yet know about my range—or lack of—culinary skills, but he must have suspected the truth, for which I was, and remain, truly thankful.

However, he had a rival waiting for him who had no intention of being displaced without a battle to the death. Romeo simply couldn't bear any attention being diverted away from himself when he chose to grace my flat with his presence. By then, I had started bathing him once a week. I would immerse him in a bucket of warm water with scented soap and scrub off the grime and petrol stains with a long-handled brush, while Romeo did his best to rip my arms to pieces. I would then dry him, powder him with Pond's Dreamflower talc, and then release him—at which he would shoot over the garden wall—ripe, smelling of rich food and of course, become the natural target of all his rivals, who were eaten up with envy, as well as masses of fleas.

As expected, he took extreme umbrage to Antonio establishing himself as a member of the household and immediately went on a hunger strike. It was a hunger strike *in situ* too, because as much as he loathed Antonio, he couldn't bear to stay away and let this in-house rival make any more headway. This went on for two terrible weeks, while Romeo got thinner and thinner, I felt more and more distracted and more and more fried mackerels languished, smelly and uneaten, left in untouched plates on the kitchen floor.

One evening, when we were in the sitting room peacefully reading and listening to Mozart, Romeo, after an absence of an entire day, slunk through the open door to the garden. 'My darling!' I cried, and gathered him into my arms, at which he savagely snarled and sunk his teeth into my forearm. This injury was too much for Antonio, having made many, many affectionate overtures over the past week to Romeo, and who, in turn, had retaliated by rubbishing his clothes and peeing on them. At other times, when Antonio would attempt to cradle him in his arms, he would just close his eyes wearily into icy green slits and sick up on his shirtfront, as if to say—You simply disgust me.

'You think you come from the bush?' roared Antonio, grabbing Ro by the scruff of his neck and glaring into his eyes, eyeball to eyeball, 'Well, I come from it too, and that's the African bush, not your piddling backyard.' And with that, he flung the astounded (and silent) Romeo into outer darkness. We heard the thump as he landed heavily, and the shrieks of outrage as he vowed vengeance. I cried as Antonio washed and spread iodine on my wounds.

Romeo didn't appear for a whole two days. On the evening of the third (which I had spent berating Antonio for his cruelty to a helpless and rightfully jealous cat, who thought I was his sole property), we were once again in the sitting room. However, the atmosphere was far from peaceful, for Antonio, twice as tender-hearted as I am about animals, was tortured by visions of the hapless Romeo—sick with love, beaten up by one of his rivals in his weakened state, or run over or simply fading away under some tree, too many streets away. Like the Cheshire cat, Romeo suddenly jaunted through the garden door.

Some people never learn. Once again, I jumped up and called lovingly to him. While shiftily looking at me, sidestepping my clutching arms, Ro made an evasive circuit of the room, finally sidling over to Antonio's chair. He then jumped up on to Antonio's chest and laid his mangy head on his collarbone, all the while gazing up moonily into his face. Clearly, he'd accepted defeat at the hands of a worthier rival for once in his life. He had also acquired a second—and even more attentive—slave. From then on, as Antonio was and is a marvellous cook, Romeo relived the good old days of gourmet cuisine being taken for granted with my mother around. The fishmonger was in heaven. This is not to say that Romeo was afraid of widening his palate—his rasping purr when he was handed a pot of freshly made chicken liver *pâté* by Antonio was like a whole sawmill in full swing.

When we moved to a bungalow just ten minutes away from our flat, the first thing I moved was Romeo. I sat in an autorickshaw with Ro in a basket, next to our maid clutching at least six packets of gradually melting butter. Of course, I had fallen for that old wives' tale about buttering a cat's paws when he entered a new home so he would stay in it. I had not fully realized Romeo's passionate devotion to his own stamping ground and his determination never to leave it to be ruled by a lesser cat.

It took him five minutes to bolt down the road, leaving a rich trail of best butter behind him.

All our old neighbours were then alerted. Twice we received triumphant calls, announcing that they had Romeo locked in their kitchens, at which point we would drop everything, rush over, and bring the warrior 'home'; but it was a location he was determined not to accept as such, for he was gone as soon as he'd eaten breakfast, lunch and dinner at one go. Finally, after hours spent peering with a flashlight into garbage cans and underbrush in vacant lots ('Yes, I heard Romeo's voice an hour ago'), we unhappily decided to leave things be for a while; we also needed an uninterrupted night's sleep.

Three weeks later, we received another phone call ('I have him locked in my bathroom, and he looks awful'), and 'rescued' a cat who was almost skin and bones, and had obviously spent a lot of time under a car, as he was streaked with oil stains.

'We've got him this time!' we said triumphantly to each other, as Romeo ate his way ravenously through mounds of food and then collapsed, sated, on our bed and started to snore. I didn't even try to clean him up. He stayed with us for three days, eating like a truckdriver, until he was as sleek as a louse and his stomach almost touched the floor. Then, one evening, as we were getting dressed to go out, he jumped lightly onto the windowsill, turned to us, said, 'parp!' and vanished into the twilight.

That was really goodbye.

After a night of crying and chain-smoking, I knew the time had come at last. I still had a partner, and we had a garden, small though it was.

It was time to get Joshua.

The Birth of an Obsession

EVERYTHING HAPPENED IN DARKNESS.

As soon as we moved, we asked a good friend who showed dogs and loved them (in fact, he collected them, and his mother looked after them) to look out for a male blue-roan cocker spaniel pup for us. Barely a week after Romeo's defection, Satish called one evening, said he'd found what we wanted and that the pups were ready to leave the kennel. We got into an autorickshaw (although I had managed to pass my driving test once I'd arrived in Bangalore, such was the chaos on the streets that neither Antonio nor I were anxious to join the traffic) and headed for an unfamiliar part of town.

The owner of the kennel came out with two pups cradled in his arms. We could barely see them, the streetlamps were very dim—later we realized why he would have otherwise also been reluctant for us to explore his premises. He explained that there were four puppies in the litter, two boys and two girls, and he'd only brought out the boys as that was what we wanted.

Each of us took a handful ... the pups were only three weeks old and barely fitted into an average sized hand; fitting into my palm (like a kernel in a nut) was Joshua, his little body collapsed against mine in total trust. I breathed in deeply the scent I'd been so homesick for; homesick for over twenty years: the warm, biscuity, vanilla scent of baby's skin and breath. Mine, all mine, to have and to hold, till death did us part.

I should have been shouting in triumph at this end to such a long journey towards getting a dog of my own, but in fact I was simply dissolving in this love—huge, sloppy oceans of it. Antonio held his brother, who would have looked sad by comparison if he didn't look so funny. He was milk-white, with black markings placed at random, almost as a joke: one over an eye, on an elbow, lopsided on his bottom, a speckled stomach.

Although I longed to take Josh home, I thought he was far too tiny to be parted from his mother. 'Can't he stay until he's eight weeks old? I'll come to see him every day. We'll pay you extra,' I said. But the kennel owner was adamant—by his iniquitous system, the pups were weaned at eighteen days and sold at twenty-one. In fact, the other three in Joshua's litter were already booked, and were leaving for Chennai the very next day.

'In any case, you'll feed him better than anything he'll get here, so take him if you want him.'

The horrible man handed over Josh's certificate of pedigree (it was certainly larger than the puppy), and took Brother away from Antonio, who relinquished him reluctantly—'Can't we keep him, too?'

'No!' I said.

Josh's official name, according to the Kennel Club of India, was Ajax. He was born on 12 December 1998. His sire's name was Champion Ponside Magic Flute, and his dam's Ponside's Temptress. He was descended, among others, from Hanna Henrietta Florentina Von Lalitken and Champion Von Jagsburgs's Jojo of Ushan.

We wanted to meet both his parents, but only his mother belonged to the kennel. The owner went inside and returned carrying a skeleton. What had once been an exquisite little '*papillon*' (butterfly) cocker spaniel, with traditional red and black markings upon the white fur, and silky streams of 'feathers' (which is what the hair on the legs is called) had every bone protruding through her dulled coat and could hardly lift her head. Although she was barely three, her owner said proudly, he'd had three litters off her already. I forcefully prevented Antonio from grabbing Joshua's mother away from the beast. The beast stood firm—he refused to sell her to us at any price. All the way home, with Joshua wrapped snugly in my best wool shawl, Antonio mourned.

A year and a half later, when I was at our one and only dog show with Joshua, we met this latter day Simon Legree again. He congratulated me on how well Josh had 'turned out', and I asked after his mother. Of course, the poor little lady, little Ponside's Temptress, was dead—dead from producing puppies at an assembly line. I had already reported him to the SPCA, but they had had numerous similar complaints and too few volunteers to deal with them.

Joshua was conceived at a heavy price, like many others.

Antonio and I often speculate as to what type of homes his brother and sisters found: we hope they are half as happy as our own has been for Josh, if not for ourselves. In fact, we try to fight out of his earshot, because he gets terribly distressed at even a voice raised in anger (as opposed to a voice raised to offer food, walks or song, all of which are welcome twenty-four seven).

Joshua came home to La Emeraude, as our bungalow was fancifully called. It was in a quiet part of Bangalore, still in Cooke Town—the old cantonment or army area—one of the few remaining bastions of sanity in a quiet retirement town rapidly being transformed into the IT capital of India, with all the attendant eyesores: apartment buildings, malls and the resulting, ear-splitting traffic jams.

In our locality, we were lucky enough to still have little lanes shaded by gulmohar trees, heavy with canopies of scarlet blossoms all summer; ancient rain trees with puffs of candy pink flowers; multicoloured bougainvillea hedges and many little parks with their tranquil heritage bungalows surrounding them—although they were now slightly shabby, like maiden aunts surrounded by brash young nephews and nieces, progressing with office towers, growing from every direction.

The first night was a makeshift affair. After he'd inhaled a heavy dinner of apple and wheat cereal, we laid Joshua on the bed between us on a pillow. Alas, he did what all babies do. We discovered that, unlike the piggish way he ate, he was surprisingly fastidious about personal hygiene and hated to be wet or dirty.

Finally, we worked out a system at night—we rigged up a plastic laundry basket full of shredded newspaper for him to sleep on, wedging it into an armchair. This chair spent three hours on either side of our bed, because in addition to cleaning him up whenever he needed it (anguished little squeals signalled calls for help), he needed to have a finger in his mouth all night. As a baby and, I must confess, well into my teens, I sucked my own thumb. Joshua needed one of ours, and he got it—his front teeth still stick out a bit—never mind how cramped our arms were in the process.

His tail had been docked. My mother always said it was such a pity: for a dog, a tail is one of the primary ways of expressing their feelings—a happy dog has a waggy tail. For Josh, who was happy all day long, this meant that practically the whole of his small body was constantly in motion, his rear end bopping from side to side almost continuously as he tried to wag the tail he didn't have.

He was too small to bark yet—in addition to continuously talking to him, we used to perch him on a table or a bench and, putting our faces close to his, make noises to entertain him. His favourite—it never failed to baffle him—was the aeroplane noise, which we became experts at. As the engines revved up (Antonio and I worked up a neat little duet) and the wheels started spinning down the runway, Josh's eyes would grow bigger and bigger in amazement. He would cock his head to one side and keep tilting it acutely to fathom this mystery. Often, he toppled over sideways and lay there, kicking his short legs to share in the joke.

Feeding time was an endless joy. We would place Josh on the kitchen counter with his bowl of Cerelac in front of him. He would plunge his entire face into its depths, snorts of pleasure emerging like bubbles, down to the last, precious drops. It was a constant temptation to overfeed him, but here we came up against the local vet, Dr Hemant, who, acting virtually as the FBI or the KGB, was determined to save us from ourselves—not to mention the fat fees he pocketed for every trifling ailment we thought Josh was suffering from. He would undertake surprise visits at odd hours of the day, and if he caught us at the bowl and counter bit outside of regular mealtimes, or if we hadn't had time to wipe off Joshua's face, we were in for it.

I have to say that Antonio, a truly inventive cook, ruled in the kitchen at that point, as I still hadn't progressed much beyond my expertise with the microwave.

When Josh was not yet two months old and was still restricted to Cerelac, Antonio and I had a little picnic celebration one evening with all our favourite foods.

We started with samosas, moved on to asparagus vinaigrette, continued on to devils on horseback and were just starting on the carpaccio when Antonio looked down and saw Josh squealing like a spotted piglet at our feet, maddened by all the wonderful smells. He tore off a small piece of the carpaccio and offered it to Josh, who almost bit his finger off.

From that moment on, all he wanted was meat. At dinnertime, instead of diving for the cereal bowl on the counter, our boy dug in his heels and refused to cooperate. When we pushed his mouth down into the bowl, he snapped his head up and sprayed the loathed cereal out from between his teeth in a fine stream—a gesture of total contempt. Thereafter, I took my first steps in cuisine, spending painful hours chopping carrots and green beans into matchstick slivers and cooking them with the best minced beef. Josh ignored the vegetables and concentrated on the flesh.

During the summer of his first year, the heat hammered down. By a process of elimination, we discovered that the only thing he would eat for lunch was vanilla ice-cream. It was a terrible moment when Dr Hemant, on one of his surprise check-up visits, found Joshua deep in a bowl of the stuff, making little piggy noises of enjoyment, sucking it up at high speed.

'What,' thundered the good doctor, as Josh lifted his face, smeared in a white mask, 'is *that?*'

'Well,' I quavered, 'Doctor, you know ... it's so hot and ... he's so stubborn ... he won't eat anything but ice-cream, and we were getting so worried he would starve and ...'

'Let him starve!' roared Dr Hemant, 'It will do him no end of good! Just you see what I'll do if I catch you giving him any of that stuff again. Ice-cream! I've never heard of such a thing! And every *day?*'

The oracle had spoken; if we did fall from grace occasionally, we made sure it was far from home, where the doctor couldn't see the three of us indulging in forbidden vice.

When Josh was much older, this same vet came into the kitchen unexpectedly one morning and saw, ranged on the counter, vitamins, mineral oils, calcium supplements and iron supplements.

'What,' boomed Dr Hemant, 'are *those?*'

Trembling, I explained that these were all the things *he'd* said Josh had to have every day.

'I said until he was *six months old*! He's over a year now—what are you trying to produce? Superdog?'

I have to admit that the vitamins worked. We can spank Josh till the palms of our hands are blood red, and he simply seems to laugh—building up muscle does it every time.

However, we've moved ahead of ourselves, and as the Victorians have said, we anticipate.

The local grocery store did deliveries, but one day I had to go by for emergency supplies. The grocer glanced at my waistline, and with a puzzled look, asked me if by any chance we had a baby in the house.

'No,' I replied, laughing.

'But, Madam,' Mr Basha said, 'every day you are using up nearly one packet of Cerelac—all twelve flavours you have used over and over already!'

When I told him that we did indeed have a baby—a four-legged one—at home, his eyes went as round as saucers.

Clearly, these two artists were crazier than the neighbourhood had imagined!

But my malady had begun a long, long time ago.

Other Boys, Other Times

AS A TEENAGER, WHEN THE HUMAN BOYS I BEGAN TO DATE CAME TO FETCH me at home, they had to sit through agonizing—for them—recitals of 'and he said to me this morning/afternoon/evening and then he did …' while the hero of the story sat between us on the sofa, proud head erect, his paw firmly on my knee, making it very clear who belonged to whom. Occasionally, my mother—whatever she felt about the swain in question—would call me out of the room and hiss, 'For God's sake, will you stop talking about that dog?'

'But,' I would answer, 'what would I talk about then?' The centre of my universe was already established. These poor souls (according to my younger sister Sunita, who still dines out on stories of me) were anyway only encouraged by me because Brandy, the cocker spaniel we had at the time, had a passion for taking drives in flashy cars, and he was pretty sure that when a young man turned up at our door, he'd have his father's car keys clutched in his sweaty hand.

And he did ... when we left the house, it was a date *à trois* ... Brandy would jump smartly into the front door, held open for me, and plant himself on the spotless upholstery, while I got in the back. The boyfriend's bleat of, 'But can't he sit on the floor? And why in the front?' received a stern reminder, 'Of course he can't see out of the window properly unless he sits in the front, and as for the floor—'

Meanwhile, Brandy had his whole head out of the window, glorious champagne coloured ears flying in the breeze, occasionally shouting joyously, while I kept my eyes dreamily on the expression upon his face. Boyfriend drove grimly on ... '*Again*, around the park?' Of course, again around the park, if he wanted to see me again—and most generally did. That is, if they could manage to part me from my shadow, 'No, the Yacht Club does *not* allow dogs! No, I'm *not* shouting. Now, for just once—'

Brandy was a darling, but he spent nearly all his time in the arms of Morpheus instead of mine, and he was also desperately vain and his waking hours were spent grooming his snow-white chest. Strangely, unlike most cocker spaniels, who are water dogs, he loathed being bathed. I had to do this with him sitting on my lap, pouring water over my head as he held my waist in a death grip, moaning into my chest. He had none of Joshua's exuberance, nor Josh's sharp appetite for pleasure that made his rollercoasting hedonistic ride so much fun, indigestion be damned.

Time rolled on and I was, to everyone's surprise (including my own), earning my own living at the age of twenty-one, in the star shaped city of Paris, France.

Bleak country indeed—hardly a sniff of a dog—nearly every one of them shut in cruel apartments. The few sightings

I had on the pavements made me feel like a shipwrecked sailor spotting a sail.

Of course, at first there was Oswaldo. I had immediately taken a babysitting job on the beautiful Ile St. Louis, an island sailing like a swan in the middle of the Seine, because as soon as my prospective employer, Madame Goudino, opened the door, I saw dear Oswaldo—a dun coloured cocker, with his head slumped drearily on his paws in the corner of the room. Our eyes met and I silently promised him better things to come.

Madame Goudino, stick-thin, red-haired and neurotic, had a son. He was a pale brat of three, called Artur, who spent his time alternately throwing up or holding his breath till his face turned green. I didn't blame him—the apartment was a nightmare. All the walls were lacquered in black and the floor was red. The furniture was all in circular pieces of taupe suede; Madame's second husband (and the father of Artur) was an Italian designer—the décor was his, and so was Oswaldo, whom he loved. But Madame did not. I was horrified to see that she fed him an unvaried diet of boiled rice. No wonder he was depressed!

I immediately accepted the job (despite painful conversations over lunch about stereotypical ideas of Calcutta and the surprising fact that I seemed to be civilized; in fact, almost like *her*) and itched for Madame to leave the apartment so I could get my hands on Oswaldo. The minute the door clanged shut, we leapt into each other's arms. Making sure that Artur was properly occupied: had a plastic basin close to hand (useful for either end) and that the cleaning lady was with him, I would put Oswaldo on his leash and we would rush down three flights of stairs to the glorious spring afternoon unrolling before us ... past the plane trees in full radiant leaf, down the steps to the quay for a good gallop along the waterfront, while gazing upon the gothic splendour of Notre Dame. Then, with the meagre wage they paid me, I would buy huge cornets of French fries or bags of madeleines—the little cakes Proust loved—and we would sit on the steps of the quay an hour later and share them. Fortunately, I was staying with generous friends of my family, the Moreaus, and could afford to spend everything on the deserving.

Madame Goudino was puzzled by my willingness—nay, eagerness—to babysit for free in the evenings. Actually, it was the only time I could really cook a proper meal for Oswaldo, when they went out to whatever esoteric amusement they favoured: plays translated from the Namibian, Chinese opera or the latest exhibition of incomprehensible installations in steel-wool and toilet-paper. I would put Artur in his room and Billie Holliday on the player—Oswaldo was a great softy and felt sentimental along with her—her life had been as sad as his. Monsieur Goudino (who actually was rather dishy in a dark, piratical sort of way) was too busy making leather bondage garments to walk Oswaldo and I'm sure he had no idea what his jealous wife fed him.

I would then set about cooking the meat I'd brought with me. I had no more idea than Oswaldo about how to prepare it, so I simply chopped it all up, put some peeled vegetables over it and sloshed some of Mr Goudino's red wine after it—*premier cru*, nothing but the best for the poor love. After he'd devoured his dinner, chasing the dish around the kitchen down to its last morsels, I would push all the strange suede pieces of furniture together, and we would lie down; Oswaldo's head would be on my shoulder and we would share a big bar of chocolate and sing along to Julie London (much happier now).

Of course, we were caught red-handed after a couple of months when they came back early and surprised us both in *flagrante delicto*, with the sound of Artur's wailing drowned by Ella Fitzgerald and I was thrown out. I missed Oswaldo more than I can say and would look up at the apartment building where he was once again imprisoned whenever I went for walks on the Ile St. Louis.

Many years later, watching Joshua romp through his golden days with such infectious *joie de vivre*, I often thought of Oswaldo and wished he could have enjoyed some of the pleasures that Josh takes so much for granted. We are his slaves and we jump to every barked command, or there could be hell to pay.

By coincidence, one morning in Paris, Madame Goudino and I met on a bus, and I asked after Oswaldo. 'I notice you do not mention my son,' said Madame coldly and I thought, what the hell, and told her it must have been obvious to anyone who I cared for more.

I promoted myself, from babysitting to actually running a language school five years later, and at our third location, I hit pay dirt. After changing addresses twice, the school was finally established in the now fashionable *quartier* of the Marais on the right bank, and the dogs had come out in force. Here, a lot of people were either rich and didn't need to work, or else they ran small boutique-style businesses where a dog in the shop was a cachet instead of a liability. The giant Scotch terrier called Batman, the batty Irish setter called Beau, the dachshund called Daddy-Long-Legs (*daddee-daddee*)—they all eventually found their way to my office, where they were sure to get hot milk from the coffee machine and unlimited biscuits from a special tin I kept.

I shall never forget the day that I looked up from the accounts I was making (yes, I learned to do them almost by osmosis—but, I have since forgotten every computation I managed and today a balance sheet might well be written in Swahili for all I understand of it) to see a wet nose pressed against the glass door to my small office, with a little mist of steam around it. I jumped up, opened the door and saw before me the most adorable basset hound puppy—a velvety mix of ivory and umber.

An hour later, I was still doing my accounts, but with the puppy now draped across my bosom and his head on my shoulder, smelling deliciously of milk, snoring softly, his belly full of best rich tea mixed biscuits from Marks and Spencer.

There was a sudden and unholy commotion going on in the courtyard—lots of shouting, the sound of pounding footsteps and then, on the other side of the glass door, a dishevelled, elderly blonde lady goggling in amazement.

The next minute, she had flung open the door and had begun to shriek, 'Orchidé! Orchidé!'

Of course, that had to be his name, 'little Orchid'. It suited him so well. Little Orchid, rudely awoken by the noise, lifted his head, opened his eyes wide, saw his legal mistress, opened his mouth, unfurled a long pink tongue in a yawn and settled his adorable head back on my shoulder. In time, Orchidé's mistress and I, though we never became what is called close, at least let the bugles ring truce. When he escaped, she at least knew where he was, though she eventually managed to persuade me to substitute plain digestives for the rich tea.

And so it went on, dog-less days interspersed with brief periods of bliss when I had my arms around someone else's dog.

Catherine, the friend whose room I'd shared when I was first in Paris, used to shout at me when I kissed their family dog, a big black Pyrenean sheep dog called Rana. 'Not on the mouth, Tanya! Not on the mouth—are you crazy? And nobody calls a dog "*mon chéri*"—everyone will think you're madder than you actually are!'

Twenty years later and after I'd moved back to India, I came to visit and Catherine drove to meet me in the south of France. She had four children by then, but the front seat was occupied by a majestic biscuit coloured Labrador. As soon as Catherine got out of the car, she released him and fell on his neck, 'Natal, are you okay? *Mon chéri*, are you feeling sick?' After she'd assured herself that her beloved was *compos mentis* (the children were still locked in the car), she turned to me and at my open-mouthed look of amazement, said sheepishly, 'Everyone changes, Tanya, even me!'

It was clear that we were on the same page at last.

The Age of Joshua

IT HAD BEEN A LONG HAUL BETWEEN HAVING THAT COCKER SPANIEL gazing mournfully from a plate on the shelf in my sitting room in Paris and touching the real thing, but it had been worth the wait. The heartbroken gaze that a cocker spaniel can switch on at the drop of a hat: those enormous, soulful eyes filled with the sorrow of all the world, framed by long, drooping ears, is a complete put-on. Looking like Elizabeth Barrett Browning in a trance is one of their favourite ruses to make the opposition crumble.

Apart from the neurotic fringe, they are some of the most fun-loving creatures on the planet and that very look, together with the insistent scrape of the paw on your knee, is only when they want a treat or most of whatever you're eating. What I particularly adore about this breed are their jowls. Try kissing a fox terrier on its sharp muzzle, and then contrast it with the velvety feel of a cocker's cheek. There simply isn't any competition.

Of course, baby Joshua was the toast of Cooke Town. In the interest of honesty, I must admit that this popularity was mostly because, at this point, he wasn't very mobile (in fact, could barely waddle from lap to lap) and he hadn't yet learned to bark. The trouble began when he began to do both, and that too with a vigour that left our friends' wine glasses, snacks and persons in permanent danger, and their ears ringing to boot. Josh became hyperactive and developed a nice tonal colour, coupled with extraordinary lung power—when denied or wanting something, he could go on without drawing a breath for hours, until he got what he wanted. For a fairly small dog, he had a positively Pavarotti sound.

But, for the moment, he was a moppet. Every morning, the fruit lady would come by with the little wooden cart, loaded with bananas, pineapples, papayas, oranges, sweet limes (which taste rather like a cross between a grapefruit and an orange) and I would ferry Josh over the garden gate. After smacking many kisses on his large head and spitting over her shoulder (to ward off the evil eye), she would place him on the cart and peel a little butter banana, which he would eat politely, if slushily. More kisses, more spitting and then the handing over again.

Like all puppies, he would have furious bursts of energy—generally after a meal—and rush around like a little black and white bullet, before suddenly collapsing in a heap and falling soundly asleep on the spot.

Naturally, we took him everywhere with us. By this time, we'd made many friends in that hospitable city ... we had met many artists, architects and like-minded people; the writer Anita Nair was Joshua's godmother and Viki Sardesai, a brilliant designer, was his godfather. Everyone got used to the sight of us arriving at a lunch or dinner party, a wine or cheese tasting or a literary evening, carrying my famous green wicker basket. After perfunctory greetings to the company, we would then immediately start unloading the basket. First, newspapers (we subscribed to three a day, none of which we actually read) which we would start spreading over the floor. Then came the bowl of Cerelac and another of water, and finally, the miracle child himself—with his red blanket (actually, a beautiful thick muslin scarf belonging to Arunesh, which Josh had appropriated and would wrap himself in to sleep when he had finally exhausted all the entertainment on offer).

And a pattern was set, and it persisted. Josh regarded an outing as a short drive to a gathering of jolly people, where he would eat and drink to his heart's content and then go home immediately afterwards. If we showed a tendency to linger—that is, after we'd swallowed the last mouthful of dessert—he would start barking. And barking. And barking. As one of our friends bitterly said when I asked what we should bring for dinner the other day—now that Josh is going on fifteen—'Just a sedative for your dog, and try to give him a good strong dose before you bring him—since you refuse to get him a muzzle.'

But he was irresistible. There is nothing like the milky-sweet smell of a puppy, and I inhaled it all day, making up for all those barren years without it. There is nothing like the joy of having this living, breathing little bundle in the crook of my arm as I slept—and to wake up with him and his yawn in anticipation of a new day, his eyes brighter every minute.

As he grew, he never really grasped the concept of the newspaper. When, at the first sign of him commencing to pee, I would lift him and place him on the paper, he thought it was a game. Finally, he decided it was some sort of fixation, and when he peed, he would place an unsteady paw, or part of a paw, on the paper, pee copiously on the floor and look up at me as if to say, 'I'm satisfying the letter of the law—just to please you, mad as it looks.'

By the time he was three months old, he was at least house-broken—or house *and* garden-broken. Since we had started taking him for short walks, in the course of which he did his business, it became his fixed conviction that any business had to be done outside the front gate. We have to take him out, as often as he wants, day or night, so as not to pollute the sacred home.

Habits are dangerous things. Sometimes he really needs to go. Sometimes he's had a long nap in the evening and feels the need to have a frolic outdoors at 2 a.m. I have to say, years later, when I am alone with him, a good shout, followed by a good whack on the bottom (if called for) is enough to settle him until daybreak. But he realized very soon that Antonio was a pushover. Even if it is four times a night, he heaves himself out of bed and takes Josh out. When we lived in Goa, he often had to chase him around the garden, swearing hoarsely, until he had collared and brought him back to bed. When we moved to the mountains, the cold made these night-time sorties a special form of torture.

Because, of course, he still sleeps with us. Generally, heavy across my feet, so that I wake up feeling like I've run a marathon. Sometimes, with his head against my shoulder, both snoring gently in unison. Often sprawled luxuriously and diagonally across the rest of the bed on his back, with his paws crossed on his chest, so that Antonio, coming to bed later, feels compelled to sleep on the sofa—'I didn't want to wake him, he looked so comfortable.' Well, more the fool he, I have to say, though Josh no doubt appreciated his delicacy.

My sister Sunita often remarked, not without a certain edge, that it was so unfair that I, having whooped it up in Paris for all those years, came back to India to find a dog, and instead, had a man fall into my lap—and he cooked, sewed, fixed things, gave massages and even ironed my panties. (This was done for my friends as well.) Of course, there was a price to pay. Antonio's adjustment to permanently living in India wasn't easy. Even if I'd never worked in India, I had been born and brought up there—coming back was like slipping into a pair of comfortable old slippers. The transition from the New to the Old world was very rocky for Antonio. Fiery and volatile, he didn't take easily to the snail's pace at which things got done, nor to the closed-shop aspect of the local art scene, and neither to the social conventions his life had hitherto been free of. He would have outbursts of anger, during which he would pace around the room, arms flailing like windmills, and give voice to his discontent at top volume.

In this, Joshua was my ally. Both of us wanted peace at any cost, and we hated any form of violence—verbal or otherwise. Noise we loved, as long as we were making it (in speech or in song, but definitely not the noise of distress). Josh couldn't bear Antonio and myself to be at odds. When we did raise our voices in anger, Josh would sit there, his head moving from one to the other as we argued, like a spectator at a tennis match. Naturally, he understood every word.

When Antonio had worked up to his climax, I was subjected to his famous 'I've had enough, I'm going to get on an international flight tomorrow!' And I would reply, 'Good! I'm so glad I bought that new suitcase; you can take it with you.' Josh would produce a heartrending howl, and we would stop in our tracks and fling ourselves upon him, pick him up and assure him that nobody was leaving. It always took us a while to convince him that we really meant it. We tried to stop fighting—or at least, to stop fighting when Josh was in earshot, which reduced our possibilities significantly. He simply couldn't bear any sounds of discord or unhappiness; they would shake the foundations of his whole conception of the universe. You could say that Joshua saved our relationship from exploding practically every day!

One morning, Antonio and Joshua were dropping me off to 'Silver Moon', when we passed our neighbours, Rustum and Connie's house. Connie, her face set in grim determination, was standing in the porch, surrounded by cartons, suitcases and her new and beloved microwave.

'I've had enough!' she replied to our question regarding what was going on, 'I'm leaving that bastard for good.' We persuaded her to wait until that evening, when they could both come over to our place and we could talk things through. That they had six dogs that they both adored had something to do with our eagerness to help as well.

It turned out to be an evening of true confessions. As Connie poured out her woes, voice rising ever higher, Joshua got more and more agitated. By the time she burst into tears, he was sitting on her lap and frantically licking the tears off her cheeks, crooning with shared anguish and pawing at her—as if to stop her crying to become the cheerful and super-efficient soul he had known from babyhood.

Rustum was no fool, either. He gathered the heaving Josh into one arm and put the other around Connie. 'Please,' he said, 'I'm so sorry. I promise I'll try harder. Look at Joshua—he won't stop crying unless you do. Come, come, let's be friends again.'

Tears were dried, drinks were poured all around; Josh the marriage counsellor had done it again! Those six dogs would continue to have a mother *and* a father. The Bible does not say 'blessed are the peaceable' but 'blessed are the peace-makers'. Rowdy and brash he may be, but Josh, in his own way, did his bit to keep the peace.

It is lucky that neither Antonio nor I ever yearned for children. Both of us are blessed with several godchildren, in various parts of the world, and we often sighed over the dream of a little girl who stayed six forever, without really ever meaning it. However, this lack of children is probably all for good, because any child of ours would have been spoiled rotten. Besides, after Joshua arrived on the scene, any child's nose would have been well and truly put out of joint!

My focus was—and remained—Joshua, but Antonio naturally gravitates towards *any* animal, and his soft heart (so steely with the two-legged in general) was daily wrung by any animal in distress. When he went to posh art camps at five-star hotels in Mumbai or Delhi, the staff grew used to the sight of Antonio lying on the hotel lobby's floor with the so-called 'guard dogs' in his arms, involved in a joyous wrestling match. To the despair of their trainers, he would raid the breakfast table and slip them goodies every morning, saving some for street dogs outside as well.

Luckily, our garden was tiny, so I was easily able to dissuade him from collecting abandoned calves, stray goats and probably half the neighbourhood mongrels.

But there are always exceptions.

The Advent of Saint Thomas

WHEN JOSH WAS AROUND SIX MONTHS OLD, I WENT OUT ONE EVENING to buy chicken rolls for our dinner. The narrow street around the corner was crowded and the nightly vegetable market, held on the pavement, was in full swing. I was waiting in a queue for my rolls, when suddenly, I was hit in the ribs with enormous force. Simultaneously, I found my wrist in the grasp of a large, blonde muzzle. Not a tooth had broken the flesh. I looked down on a pair of melting, doe-shaped, amber eyes and long blonde eyelashes shading them modestly. The eyes were widely set—never trust a person with close-set eyes, my grandmother Emilia had said—under the noblest of foreheads. He seemed to be a cross between a mongrel, a Labrador, and a Great Dane. Beautifully proportioned, with long finely boned legs, he was a large dog who looked as if he'd been dipped in honey all over, except for the tip of his powerful tail, which was white. His temperament was as sweet: he glowed with it as he gazed up at me.

It was love at first sight. I held my rolls in one hand; the other remained imprisoned by my new friend as he followed me home, his eyes full of light.

When we reached the house, I had to disengage myself and leave him outside the gate, because we had a problem inside.

The problem's name was Prince, and we had met, more or less, the same way as my beautiful new acquaintance. He was a coal-black mudhol hound, the kind you see in Mughal miniatures of hunting scenes, but he had a pair of ominously slanted yellow eyes. He had been meek as a lamb when he had followed me home one evening, while I was walking back from my library; but that was about a month ago. Once we had taken him into our home, he turned into a monster.

About a year old, he was certainly clever. A bit too clever. He simply couldn't understand why he, whose brain was bursting with brilliance, who was a top-quality hunting dog to boot, got so little attention while Joshua, that spoiled little no-account piddling puppy, was treated like the crown jewels. He had a way of just sitting lightly on his haunches and his sense of balance was so impressive that he had fallen twenty feet off from our terrace to the ground below, while chasing a cat, and had only suffered a lightly grazed elbow—and fixing his eyes on Josh, who would be innocently bumbling around, collecting new smells. I didn't like that expression on his face at all and was quite sure that Josh would be his breakfast or lunch one day.

Then, two things happened, and they removed Prince from our orbit and brought Thomas—as I had named him—into it. Arunesh told us that a friend of his in Delhi was going to spend a year at Harvard, and that she was sending both her dogs down to him to look after in the interim that very weekend to Bangalore and that, as his new house was quite a bit out of town and very large, he needed a guard dog. Prince was the very man for him. Meanwhile, Thomas was sitting, outside our gate—like Patience on a monument—refusing any nourishment, gazing into our house with yearning.

My mother was visiting us at the time. She, much like myself, had a healthy distrust of Prince; but one look at Thomas, sitting like a statue in the sun, and she said, 'That dog is a thorough gentleman.'

Antonio was torn between the very real desire to have Thomas be a part of our family and his weakness for the underdog, whom he mistakenly took Prince to be. By now, such was Prince's sense of empire that he allowed nobody—neither man nor animal—to approach our house. Anyone in uniform was a special enemy, and the postman lived in terror of him. He was as fast as a rattlesnake too and moved like a shadow.

I finally managed to persuade Antonio of the wisdom of avoiding homicide (in the case of Joshua) and/or court cases (in the case of everybody else on two legs, the postman already having muttered about official letters of complaint to be sent to higher personnel).

Departure Day was set for that very Friday. Possibly in order to punish me, on Friday morning, Antonio insisted I go to the much larger market in Bangalore, Russell Market, and buy a basket and two rugs for the displaced dauphin. When I returned from the library that evening, I found both of them stiff, sitting in the dining room, with Prince's water and food bowls near their feet, along with all of his new gear, accusingly watching me approach. As if I were Cruella De Vil!

This was nothing compared to his departure. Arunesh, on his way back from the airport, drew up in a jeep at 8 p.m., with his friend's mongrel and Lhasa Apso in the back. We had to stack Prince's gear inside and then manhandle him into the jeep, which then took off instantly (I had warned Arunesh to make a quick getaway, much in advance).

As his howls of protest died down in the distance, and peace descended on La Emeraude at last, we called out to Thomas. He had been waiting like a saint for a whole week in his spot below the hedge, outside the front wall.

'Come, Thomas,' I said, opening the gate. Thomas stalked in with regal dignity, entered the front door, gave Josh a kindly, brotherly look, jumped up on the sofa, crossed his front paws, and let out a heartfelt sigh of relief. He had come home at last, never to leave.

Thomas tackled the problem of bringing Joshua up with the same gentle resignation, mixed with the same philosophical depth, that he brought to our life. Joshua (although he had a substantial collection of stuffed toys) never chewed any, nor did he chew on slippers or furniture. He preferred live flesh—ours. By this time, our arms and legs were worn and ragged with love-bites from his needle-sharp baby teeth. Thankfully, he now began to sharpen his teeth on Thomas, who was not only less vulnerable than us, but also more accessible.

Many were the wrestling matches they had—Thomas, as gentle as a lion with one of his young cubs, occasionally swatted the roly-poly bundle off from his head, especially when Josh tried to shred his ears, or he held him firmly under one long, bony paw when the sport was too boisterous.

In fact, we learned that the entire neighbourhood, who had known and loved Thomas for years, called him 'Lion', because of his size, his colour and his eyes. He had been fed by dozens of them at their gates, but would never enter their houses, no matter how hard they had tried to entice him. He had chosen us, and whatever his inscrutable reasons might have been, for that we are forever grateful.

The only thing that marred his beauty was a huge scar that ran from the middle of his forehead down to his nose. As he was as gentle as a gazelle (and as clean, I might add, relative to Joshua), life on the streets must have been very hard at times.

Dr Hemant, the vet, announced that he must be about four-years-old, judging from his teeth. Although he'd never been examined before, he opened his mouth on command and held it open as long as was needed, with one long, elegant, slightly trembling paw laid trustingly upon my knee.

We never ceased to feel blessed that he had condescended to join our family. There was never any lessening of courtesy in his manner to us; he never demanded anything or even gently asked, but the leap of joy with which he greeted an invitation to eat, or go for a walk or a drive, is proof enough that he *did* want things. He just didn't think it polite to ask.

All my girlfriends wanted a partner like Thomas; all our dog-loving friends just wanted to take him home (something you could never say of their attitude towards Joshua). But his devotion to us never wavered all his life long. As for his 'younger brother'—he regarded him with resignation, as a burden to be borne, as an occasional playmate, and mostly, a damned nuisance, though he was too civilized to say so. For his part, Joshua, who has always and totally ignored anything on four legs, made an exception for Thomas. Moreover, he worshipped him, as a divinity whose graciousness was far above dealings with messy human beings, and Josh regarded himself as one.

There is no doubt that Joshua was full of the devil. But then, the devil is unfortunately easy to relate to. Most women like the bad boys, the flashy men—even my mother, a wonderful teacher throughout her life, said she had preferred teaching the naughty boys because they were brighter, not to mention more fun. Thomas, of course, was a saint. But, while you admire and revere saints, it's difficult to connect with them on a daily basis—unless you're one yourself. They are twice-born, mysterious souls. And that Joshua certainly wasn't.

He was utterly transparent. Overindulgence in all the good things of life was his creed, whether it was food, love, travel or company. Compared to all the other dogs I'd known, his every desire was written plainly on his face, every feeling immediately expressed.

It became increasingly obvious each day, as Josh grew from puppyhood to adolescence—it was a proud moment when Thomas taught him to pee, lifting a leg without falling over backwards—that he had some springer spaniel blood. He was smaller than the average cocker, and his black and white coat was light and silky. He was too beautiful for words, but words were actually the last things we used, by now having invented an entire new language with which to talk to Joshua, made up of baby-talk interspersed with jabberwocky.

After any special treat, Josh would jump up onto a sofa or a bed, fling the cushions around in high spirits, and then lie on his back and pedal furiously in the air, panting happily all the while. There was never any furtiveness or beating about the bush with him: he was a hundred per cent present in every moment.

And he made us laugh … how he made us laugh!

Often, when I'd be holding Josh on my lap and singing to him and kissing him, Antonio (who was scrupulously fair) would point at Thomas and say, 'Look at the way he's watching you! Why don't you give him a kiss too; after all, he's the one who chose you!'

I leave the answer to Pascal, who said that the heart has its reasons, and that reason has nothing to do with it.

A coda to the saga of Prince was that, a year after he left us, we were invited to a party at Arunesh's house; it was now, because of the fearsome Prince, known as 'the house of the black dog' (a dangerous colour to be in south India, and the source of much superstition). He had very little work as a guard dog, as no one was foolhardy enough to even cross the public road in front of the house.

Antonio, ever hopeful, insisted on taking Joshua with us to visit; he said that Prince must be missing him. He also cooked a huge casserole of *boeuf bourguignon* for all the dogs to celebrate their reunion. I was sceptical but went along with the plan.

When we arrived at Arunesh's house, all the dogs streamed out to meet us, with Prince breasting the tide. He fell on Antonio like a brother, and then his yellow eyes spied Josh and I bringing up the rear. With a savage snarl that unfurled his entire armoury of white teeth, he sprang at Josh like a panther. I just had time to grab Joshua and lift him above my head before Prince struck. There was absolutely no doubt about his intentions.

The *boeuf bourguignon* was a great success with all the dogs, although we could hear Prince's howls for revenge, all the way from the room where he was eating his portion behind safely locked doors.

It must have been very hard for him to have had vengeance snatched right out of his reach, just when all the signs had been so propitious.

Let the Go Times Roll!

IF I HAVE TO TELL THE STORY OF JOSHUA, I ALSO HAVE TO TELL THE story of ourselves.

Anyone who has been told, as Joshua was, from the day we got him at three weeks old, that he was the most precious thing in the entire world, obviously believes it. That automatically meant that *we* had to live the way he wanted to. And, if we didn't get the message, he showed us how.

He taught us what true love meant, with everything that comes with it. He would do anything for us—as long as it meant he got what he wanted first—and we would do anything for him, without that qualification. I found that to be true one morning, when Josh and I, with Thomas by our side, had gone on our regular walk. Until that moment, I had never fully realised what Joshua had come to mean to me.

As we approached the park, we were unexpectedly attacked by a pack of dogs someone had let out of the house opposite us. A Great Dane and a German Shepherd rushed towards us, followed by several smaller dogs. I grabbed Josh and held him above my head and shouted to Tom to get away, while the Great Dane jumped higher and higher, trying to tear at Josh's tender little stomach. My screams finally roused someone within the house, and they came out and managed to herd the dogs and get them back inside. Poor Thomas, peace-loving and terrified of violence, had stayed at a safe distance throughout this drama, whining in deep distress and running around the spot.

The minute I put Josh down, I heard a bus roaring up the road, which was very narrow, and on a curve—immediately towards us. I was tugging at Josh's collar when it slipped out and over his head, and he started to run across the road. The bus was almost upon us. Without a second's hesitation, I flung myself upon the tarmac, smack in middle of the path of the bus, and it screeched to a halt. There was no sign of Josh at all.

After many curses from the driver, the bus moved on. I ran across the road, my heart in my mouth, only to find Josh, that dear, brave boy, cowering in the ditch, making small, terrified squeaks. He had blood all over his chest and gazed up at me piteously. Shakily, I gathered him into my arms, sat on the ground and burst into tears. Finally, I spied an autorickshaw, hailed it, and crawled into it with Josh. Thomas loped alongside it all the way to the vet's clinic. He insisted on coming inside with us and put his paws on the examination table to watch the vet examining Josh, with a deep frown creasing his forehead. In between, he gave me pleading looks that clearly seemed to beg me to not think too badly of him for failing to protect us all. The vet didn't find a scratch on Josh but said that the Great Dane must have had a mouth injury, which explains the blood.

He told me to just take Josh home, bathe him, and give him a treat. I certainly did!

Why do small boys whine? asks an old joke. *Because they're practising to be men* goes the answer. Personally, I find the fragility of men's egos to be a real bore, but Joshua, although his whining was quite dominant, was never, ever boring. However, *he* had a very low threshold for boredom, and when balked of attention, would fling himself on his back, start combing his paws over his muzzle rhythmically and embark on a sort of operetta of moans, groans and high-pitched whistling sounds that clearly said, 'Yes, they're so busy-busy-busy, while I'm so bored-bored-bored! There he is, with that stupid brush and there she is, with that silly book and here I am, and I want to talk-talk-talk! I want a party! I want action! And all he does is—' and so on and so forth, until he would abruptly roll over, jump on my lap and shove the book aside to laugh into my face, the healthy raspberry tongue lolling crazily out of the corner of his mouth.

Generally, when he began one of these recitals, Antonio would crack first, put his painting away and fetch the leash (Joshua in seventh heaven at the sight, leaping three feet off the ground, on all fours) or pick up the ball. These ball games were a joke; once Josh caught the ball (and he would only play with adults, not with children), he simply never let go. We could grasp the ball and lift Josh off his feet, pulling from both sides, but his jaws remained clamped around it until we gave up. It was a pretty one-sided affair.

But this wasn't the case during our evenings, where we *had* to spend some time dancing together. This had started when Josh was a baby and persisted until he became a bit too heavy to carry for more than one track of an album. We'd hold him between us and dance, and Josh would produce heartfelt, sentimental sighs, and lay his cheek against ours—taking turns. Naturally, when we were surprised in the act, our visitors probably thought—well, I have no idea, but maybe they found it touching.

As I was away at 'Silver Moon' only for short periods every day, and as Antonio painted at home, Josh became addicted to our joint attention and joint affection. There was no question of leaving him with anyone without one of us being present. Of course, it was entirely our own fault, and we reaped what we'd sown so liberally.

He's never been tied up in his life.

We tried, once, to leave him at a friend's house for a brief spell while we went to an exhibition; we returned after a couple of hours to find her pale and exhausted. 'He barked,' she said limply, as Josh fell on us like a reprieved prisoner, 'He wouldn't stop barking. Then he started banging against the front door and howling. I had to walk him around the park. Round and round and round and round. We just got back ... Never again. Take him away. I'm going to bed.'

Antonio had earlier frequently painted in India, but his work was relatively unknown in this country, although by that time he had been painting for more than thirty years.

However, his career slowly began to take off and he had to make trips outside Bangalore, for shows in other cities, or to go to art camps or workshops.

The first time Antonio left home to go to Canada for a month-long spell, Joshua was completely unprepared. Antonio left in the afternoon, and I kept Josh pretty busy after, but at nightfall, I suddenly couldn't find him.

I finally traced him by the whimpering sound; he was under our bed. I had to crawl onto the floor, and there were actual tears, which had created soaking runnels down his silky cheeks. He was simply a little bundle of grief at the disappearance of his Dad and it took him days to recover his normal high spirits, though he would still eagerly rush to the door every time he heard the doorbell, hoping Antonio had come home. My wicked sister suggested that Josh's grief was due to his being deprived of Antonio's *haute cuisine* and left to the mercy of my ham-fisted culinary efforts, but I refuse to share in this cynical point of view.

Joshua, although his main love was myself, never resigned himself to Antonio's departures. Every time he saw the travelling bag emerge (Antonio stuck to his habit of travelling light), Joshua would start hiding Antonio's shoes and sandals, figuring they were the one thing he couldn't leave without. With an expression of cunning on his face, he would drag them off to some hiding place—behind the sofa or under the bed in the guest room—one by one. What gave him away every time—and how easy to read the boy was!—was that he compulsively kept checking on them, making sure, and naturally, these frequent journeys didn't go unobserved by us.

Antonio, who, of course, had been watching these furtive trips to-and-fro, would start to pack his case (removing Josh periodically from inside it) and then, having inspected the empty shoe-rack, slap his forehead and exclaim, 'Where are my shoes?' Immediately, Joshua, desperate to convince himself that they were still hidden, would rush to the hoard and fling himself on top of the pile. All was discovered.

I left home only for a couple of days during Josh's childhood, and came home to find Antonio at the stove, all sorts of exotic smells rising from the frying pan. I also noticed a bottle of dry sherry next to it.

'What's that?' I asked, 'It's time for Josh's lunch—where's his mince?'

'Well, Putzi,' said Antonio, guiltily shifting from foot to foot, 'it's just ... heh ... heh, a little treat for Josh to welcome you home ... you know, just a little calves' liver with courgettes and, you know, a little *flambée* to give it that extra touch; he's become quite fussy about his food.'

Fussy! Josh, like a true gourmand, would try anything once—as long as it was freshly cooked and new to his already sophisticated palate. He was also given an ice-cube every evening, from Antonio's drink, and one of the sounds I best remember from his babyhood was the crunching of teeth on ice.

This led to his deep disgrace one day, when all three of us were invited to dinner at a designer friend's house. First of all, Josh never drank out of his water bowl. He preferred drinking out of bowls filled with water and flower petals that I had a habit of placing on the low coffee tables at home. Our host, Jenny, had a fabulous veranda, part of which was a lily pond. Ignoring the water bowl she had kindly placed next to him, Josh galloped to the lily pond, tore aside the white lotus flowers, and drank deeply. Not content, after dessert, when Jenny was serving liqueurs in little wooden cups, Josh—fired by the bowl of fresh mango ice-cream he had just eaten—leapt lithely onto the glass dining table and, putting his snout into Antonio's cup of Cointreau, drained it to the dregs.

The next morning, he was snoring deeply from the aftermath of his debauch. I woke him rudely, 'Come on, you drunken sot! We're going to walk off your hangover!'

You can imagine he was never asked to Jenny's after that. In fact, it is a measure of our friends' affection for us that they invited us at all, given that Josh was always part of the package. However, like all besotted parents, we could see no flaw in him, so delighted were we with his continuous enthusiasm.

There is a story I read as a child and have never forgotten, about a hunter going into a forest with a gun, to shoot birds for his dinner. A magpie flies over to him, and begs him not to shoot her children, who have just grown and are nesting, deep in the woods. 'How will I know if they're your children?' asks the hunter. 'Because they're the most beautiful children in the forest,' replies the bird.

The hunter has a soft heart and takes care only to shoot the ugliest birds he can find. As he is leaving, with a brace of birds slung over his shoulder, the mother flies overhead, and bursts out screaming, 'You killed them! You killed my children!' The hunter protests that, on the contrary, he had only shot the ugliest birds he could find. 'But don't you know,' wailed the mother, 'that one's own children are always the most beautiful?'

When Joshua's first Christmas was approaching, I asked my mother for the recipes for all her famous Christmas sweets. She was astonished, but sent them to me, and for the first time in my life, truly inspired by the idea of making Josh's Christmas authentic, I began to bake. And bake. And bake. Joshua would always lick the mixing bowl afterwards and sit by the oven waiting for the finished product, occasionally barking with impatience and reaching up to thump the oven door—as if that would produce instant gratification. Of course, as Josh's waistline expanded, so did mine.

Gone were the days of the wasp waists, delicate lingerie, stockings and high heels that I had needed to sustain my role in Paris as a captain of industry, although of a very, very small boat. Instead, I took to t-shirts, shorts and flip flops and donated my entire French wardrobe to Mridula, the ravishing eighteen-year-old daughter of our friend Sunil, who was leaving India to start university in the UK. She wanted to know the story of every garment—where I had worn it and what my memories were of the time. It was a bitter-sweet feeling—handing over black cocktail dresses I would never fit into any longer; recounting parties I had been to in those costumes; shopping trips with my best friend Lavinia; remembrances of where I had bought those angora sweaters and for whom I had worn them; memories of how I had wept all over that red, evening bolero jacket or cherished the summer dress printed with poppies and cornflowers for the sake of a special evening. But now the Age of Joshua had begun and it was an age much richer than that of my Parisian escapades.

I did keep the photos of my days of glory, if only to prove to Josh that I had once been whistled at in the streets of a foreign capital. But I realized that what he needed now was a more maternal companion. It was also comforting to cling to that very idea when I was on my third 'Cooke Town Sunset.' This was an amazing drink invented by our neighbour Jitu, made of dark rum, lots of crushed ice and topped with fresh coconut juice. As the level of the drink descended, the rum would rise to the surface, tinting the coconut juice—hence producing the name of the cocktail. At one point, we were drinking the 'Sunset' at high-noon in Cooke Town and the old, bespectacled gentleman who sold fresh coconuts, bicycling around the area with strings of them draped across his handlebars, struggled to keep up with the demand.

The one person who really suffered from my radical change in image was my mother Gilda, who, at seventy, was absolutely gorgeous and always perfectly groomed. She would look sadly at my hair, which was gradually being chopped from my waist to my earlobes (I found I could no longer bear the heat), and at my non-existent waistline, not to mention my (un-made-up) face and the fact that I'd abandoned all my jewellery. She would mourn, 'But you used to be so beautiful!'

Tempus fugit.

In any case, most of the jewellery went to my little niece Mallika, who, at the age of three, was already more beautiful than I had ever been or could hope to be even if I frequented the local beauty parlour every week. This same Mallika, as she grew up, became a passionate animal lover. Before she had a dog at home, she would feed and name all the mongrels who lived around their apartment building in Mumbai. When my sister Sunita begged her not to kiss them on the mouth, she would say in all seriousness, 'But where else can they feel it, Mama?'

Every time I went to visit my own mother, I returned home with boxes of treats. One of Josh's favourites were her pan rolls, an Anglo-Indian specialty: thin pancakes stuffed with a mixture of spiced beef, rolled in semolina and then fried. One evening, we had unexpected guests, and I served the pan rolls, placing them on the coffee table. We were in the middle of a heated argument when I heard a slurping sound—Joshua was calmly sitting by the table and a pan roll was disappearing into his mouth—as if he were sucking in a strand of tagliatelle!

'Joshua!' I shouted, 'What are you doing?'

Josh, having swallowed the last of it, boggled back at me, as if to say, 'Do you need me to show you? Well, all right.'

Leaning forward, he took another one delicately by the end, and commenced to slowly hoover it down. He then sat back, cocked his head and gave me a look of prolonged suffering, which said, as plain as words, 'Now do you understand? Or do I have to do it all over again?'

We fell about laughing at the expression on his face, but the dish was removed out of his reach and placed safely on top of the piano.

Nature vs Nurture

WHAT OF THE RELATIONSHIP BETWEEN JOSHUA AND US? DID HIS arrival change things between Antonio and myself?

In fact, Antonio was crazy about animals. In a way much worse than I was, because I always had a favourite, whereas he was—almost completely—impartial to any animal who was part of our household. Brought up in the highlands of Kenya and then in Eritrea, Ethiopia, his family had always kept a menagerie of beasts that were far more exotic than the dogs, cats, guinea pigs, rabbits and ducks of my Calcutta childhood. Apart from the ordinary domestic animals, they had had a baboon in Eritrea who hated the sound of Italian and a fully grown cheetah who slept behind the sitting room sofa and didn't like being disturbed. He was also unfazed by illness and kept me calm when Josh was stung by a bee or developed what sounded like whooping cough or was simply ill from overeating. Despite the fact that Josh and I were kin, Antonio was the primary caregiver. The rest of us enjoyed the fruits.

I loved grooming Josh (as I did for Thomas as well) but Antonio went the whole hog—insisted on brushing Josh's teeth regularly (having spent a fortune on a plaque-free canine dental kit), used Q-tips to clean his ears and generally behaved like a fool of a different order than me.

As far as the old arguments about nature versus nurture go, I have to say that in terms of temperament, Joshua and I were a perfect fit—time just made us more ourselves, so to speak. It was a case of two minds with a single thought; two hearts that beat as one.

In other words, as Antonio often said bitterly, Joshua and I simply lived for pleasure. Food, drink and company (not necessarily in that order) were champagne and caviar to us. The only thing he didn't do was smoke bidis (the small, hand-rolled Indian cigarettes) as I did, and he would sneeze explosively every time he inhaled the smoke, obviously longing to join in. We were both blessed with excellent digestion and could have a sound nine hours of sleep at night and still look forward eagerly to a three hour siesta in the afternoon (so good for the complexion).

Antonio, who had a delicate stomach and was prone to insomnia, would watch the pair of us eating and drinking far too much and then laying our heads on the same pillow and drifting off to dreamland with a grim look on his face, as he prepared himself for yet another night, waiting in vain for the sandman to arrive. The only thing that woke me up in a hurry was Joshua trying to wake me, sitting on my chest, pawing at me urgently and breathing heavily into my face—the all-meat diet he insisted on could made even a dustbin smell sweet. The minute I opened my eyes—even though I'd never moved a muscle—Josh was alert. Indeed, this was a kinship that would never be severed!

He also had a timer set into his stomach. After his breakfast and his morning walk, he would bounce into the kitchen and lavish greetings on our part-time maid, Kamakshi. He would then sit patiently beside her, his expectant eyes, brimming with light, fixed upon her busy hands. Kamakshi knew it was the signal for her to have her breakfast, which of course, she would then share with 'Josuway' (as she called him), dropping pieces of tea-soaked bread into his open mouth.

None of the clocks in our house were vocal, but mysteriously and exactly at noon, our boy was back in the kitchen, barking for room service on the spot. The sound of the kettle whistling meant that tea-time biscuits had to appear simultaneously. Dinner was left to the Gods—whether he got it or not depended on the varying girth of his waistline. Naturally, if I wasn't at home, he ate well every evening.

As I have already dotingly remarked, he understood every word we said. Unfortunately, this also meant he never forgot. If I carelessly promised that I would make him a banana cake before bedtime, he'd be waiting in the kitchen, glaring at the oven, until I did so. If I said he'd have an extra walk, and proceeded to forget all about it, he'd wait a while and then fetch his leash, swinging it like a lasso until I got the message. All that conversation since he was a baby, talking to him, at him, had made the chap bilingual! Our goose was well and truly cooked. Thankfully, there were long periods when he slept, otherwise I couldn't have kept up with his pace.

A real artist, Antonio lived intensely, whether he was chopping vegetables or starting a new painting. He was like a little bombshell, whizzing around with his greying ponytail flying, exploding ideas in every direction. Life was real and life was earnest. He needed practically to be chloroformed if I wanted him to stay in one place for any significant length of time. I, on the other hand, cherished the actress' response to the interviewer's question about hobbies in *Who's Who*. She had simply replied, 'Resting.'

One of my favourite haikus by Shiki said it all:

What a splendid day!
No one in all
The village
Doing anything!

Antonio did not subscribe to this point of view at all; he simply lacked the insouciant touch that Josh and I brought to life. Like the grasshopper, we simply enjoyed it with no thought for the morrow. Antonio's view of life was dark, in total contradiction to the serenity of his work. He had little to say to most people, unlike us; we who loved company – the more the better.

'Who's at the door now?' Antonio would shout, exasperated, 'Can we never have any peace?' while Joshua and I would race to welcome yet another guest; Josh with a teddy caught en route and clamped between his teeth. When left out of any conversation, Josh would bark until he was included and complimented on his beauty, his intelligence and his sweetness.

He awoke each day with unfailing good humour and appetite for life. There was no vice in him, just unbounded enthusiasm for everything, whether for his walks in the park, the endless variety of new scents and smells, the new people he met. In fact, the sun grew rounder every day for him, and it was difficult, even when he was naughty (and that was practically all the time; orders were a joke to him) to be angry for long. He would roll over and laugh or wind his paws around our arms and lick us from head to toe, or rush and collect one of his toys and pretend to battle with it, growling ferociously and watching us out of the corner of his eye.

When he was scolded—and we had to scold him sometimes, for his own good—he would grin in a way that was more of a grimace of embarrassment, after which he would affect a nonchalant air, walking off jauntily or throwing a ball across the room. And yet, in truth, he was horribly mortified, because the bouncing ball against the wall would get more and more emphatic. Finally, the ball would hit him, and he would exaggeratedly yelp in pain. This, of course, would bring us, literally and figuratively, to our knees in order to comfort the afflicted and to promise never, never, to scold him again.

The one thing that Josh couldn't do without was love. We called him 'the love-junkie' (but aren't we all?). However, the difference between us and him was that his love was never narcissistic. Dogs are the only four-legged creatures who seem to possess the rudiments of altruism and a sense of God. They love something *outside* themselves.

Every time we returned home, even after an absence of five minutes, we were greeted as if we'd been gone for aeons: he would dash to get a stuffed toy to welcome us and fall into paroxysms of joy. We would be deafened by volleys of welcoming barks, interspersed with moans of anguish, explaining how he had missed us—all accompanied by wet, fervent and heartfelt kisses wherever he could place them. We had to pick him up and hold him tight and tell him we'd never leave him again, until he had calmed down enough to draw a breath. Who wouldn't have melted at such devotion? Every day we realised how truly we were loved.

As I watched Josh grow up, I realized that animals never do anything half-heartedly—everything is acted upon as if it were happening for the first time. He really did believe us when we told him we'd never leave him again, even if he heard it every day. His heartbreak was as sharp and his overwhelming relief as earnest every time.

Ours became the only house in town that people were willing to leave their pets at. In fact, the animals' food in our house was generally much better than what we prepared for ourselves (with whatever time we had left over). One of our friends came over one day, and having skipped breakfast, headed straight for the kitchen to see what there was to eat. She told us later that the chicken stew on the stove had been divine, only to be told that it was the boys' lunch.

Naturally, Thomas and Josh were always referred to as 'the boys' and never as 'the dogs'. In fact, Josh was mortally offended by anyone who had ever offered him a snack by dropping it on the ground. He ate it, of course, but the giver was put on his personal blacklist afterwards and was never given quite the same warm greeting.

A very tangible problem between Antonio and myself were the evenings. After a days' work at my lending library ('You call that work?' people usually said, 'I call your life a perpetual holiday!') I wanted to read. Sadly, I'm an addict. I have been known to read the telephone directory if marooned in a room with no reading material, and have read practically a book a day since I was ten. There was nothing to be done about it—I needed my fix. In all honesty, I have to admit that, of all the men I've known, Antonio has been the most accommodating of my habit and has left me alone with a book for far longer than any of the others.

But even the worm will turn.

'So,' Antonio would say wistfully (or demandingly, or angrily, depending on how bad the situation was), 'are you going to talk to me this evening? How about some conversation? How about some *communication*? Huh?'

Answer there was none, because I was actually lost in seventeenth century London, held up by the plague, or helping Anne Boleyn outwit Henry VIII or deep in the woods where Keats' nightingale sang.

I was saved unexpectedly when Josh was about six months old. We were having dinner with his godmother Anita, and their television happened to be on. We had never had one, no more than we possessed a computer or a car. Animal Planet had a programme on grizzly bears in Canada. Josh, who was sitting on a beanbag, directly in front of the screen, was suddenly transfixed by an enormous, strange animal rushing directly at him!

He barked at it in vain … the grizzly came on, opened his cavernous mouth and bared its fangs. In his haste to escape, Josh fell over backwards over the beanbag, did a somersault, landed on the floor and then bravely rushed towards the screen, determined to do battle with this ferocious enemy.

I had solved my problem. The very next day, we invested in a TV, assuring ourselves that it was 'only for Josh'.

Happy evenings followed, I could lose myself with impunity between the covers of a book for as long as I wanted, while father and son explored the beasts of the world, both feathered and furred. Life was very, very good.

Money, Money, Money

PEOPLE MAY ALSO BE CURIOUS AS TO HOW WE MANAGED TO SUSTAIN Joshua's standards of high living. Antonio had never bothered about finances. He simply painted and sold his work when he needed money. He was ridiculously generous by nature, he never needed much for himself, apart from a good bottle of wine.

As he is uninterested in technology, the computer remains as much of a mystery to him today as his chequebook does. Years on, he was under the firm impression that a cordless phone was a mobile!

I had had to deal with money every day while running the business in Paris, but it too remained a curiously abstract concept in my mind. I always had enough to live on, simply but comfortably, and my many friends had kept me well supplied with clothes, great meals and holidays.

We made a pretty pair, but no matter what the world thought about us, innocent and naive as we were, we were the perfect parents for Josh. As far as worldly goods were concerned, we had enough between us to provide for our four-legged friends, and soon Antonio, as he deserved, began to sell well. He specialized in large, abstract canvases; they evoked different landscapes and mirrored their mood—from contemplative to spiritual to emotional. He also used anything he could lay his hands on, and had a mixed-media technique—from cloth scraps to ice-cream sticks to the wrappings of my bidi packets. He never used a palette, nor did he lay out his paints in advance, and his brushes always, mysteriously, remained clean. He could paint anywhere, directly onto the canvas, which he laid out flat on any available surface.

Being a messy painter myself (I'd had two shows in Calcutta before I turned twenty-one), I used an easel, a palette, bowls for oil and turpentine or water, all of which I carefully laid out on a newspaper before I began my work; I spent far too much time cleaning my brushes. However, and despite my careful preparations, I never achieved the same results as Antonio.

I had had no time in Paris—apart from drawing from life on Sundays—to paint at all. Now, in Bangalore, Antonio, horrified by this waste of talent, found one of my old nude drawings, box framed it and hung it provocatively—bang in the centre of the dining room. 'I just want you to look at it every time you pass by. If I could draw like you,' Antonio would say, 'I'd have made a fortune already.'

But I wasn't ready yet, nor would be, not until we moved to Goa.

When I first returned to India, I had chosen Bangalore to live in because I had many old friends from Calcutta living there, as well as my sister and her family. Also, I was horrified by the metropolises of India and in any case, I didn't have the kind of money to live in any of them with any degree of comfort, even if I had wanted to.

In my first flat, my neighbour across the landing happened to be back from the US on a sabbatical, to work on her master's degree in sociology and like me, was a single woman, though much younger. She took me firmly in her capable hands as far as practical matters were concerned and took me shopping for everything I needed in her car, which she drove with the verve of Michael Schumacher.

Driving back with her after midnight, after having gone out for dinner, without a word of warning, she would suddenly reverse sharply—and at a speed of 100 km an hour—down a dark and deserted by-lane, swoop to a halt and shout, 'Boss!' into the blackness. Like magic, a bent old man would shuffle out from a doorway, a bottle of iced beer in each hand. Simultaneously, she would hand over the money and grab them; my new friend would then shoot forward again and we would refresh ourselves en route for home. I once saw her, while we were caught in a traffic jam, jump out of the car and pick up a hefty young man who had been annoying us by shouting sexist remarks through the window, by the scruff of his neck. She gave him a thorough thrashing, still holding him aloft, and then dropped him, got back into the car, and started it at the green light. Of course, I had total faith in her afterwards.

One evening, she asked me what my financial situation was. Quite blithely and proudly, I replied that in Paris, apart from the money I'd saved (only to lose) for 'Silver Moon', I'd figured out how much I needed per month to live comfortably on, and that I had enough to last me five years.

'And then?'

'Well, I have no idea. I suppose something will turn up.'

She restrained herself with difficulty from attacking me the same way she'd done to our heckler and at 10 a.m. sharp the next morning, had me at the bank, so I could invest every penny I possessed. She had saved my bacon, for at that point, foreign money investments were at an all-time high as far as interest rates were concerned, and my hard-earned cash would now be put to work instead of daily diminishing to leave me penniless in the near future.

I often thought of the path that had led me to Joshua—and to Antonio.

I suppose I could have had a dog while I was living in France, by the simple expedient of marrying a rich man. At that happy point in time—happy from the perspective of the weighing scale—I was pretty hot. Sitting cross-legged, I could count my ribs, and practically sit on my hair at the same time. There were also quite a few rich men around. As I said, I was looking pretty good.

But I couldn't bring myself to do it—what would my future son think of me for making such a cold-hearted bargain? And then, for the rich man to be a dog lover as well as being rich might be too much to expect. The future Joshua needed a dad who did more than just tolerate him. No, I decided, this was going to be something I would have to do on my own. At nearly forty, I had decided to return to India; to re-cross those miles I'd flown in the opposite direction, and this time for good, not just for Christmas.

I had planned my campaign slowly and carefully, more than a year in advance. In fact, the only people who had taken my permanent departure from French soil seriously were the income tax department, who were bewildered but thrilled at my desire to pay *all* my taxes for the current year, six months in advance. Most French people spend all their ingenuity on finding ways to avoid paying any taxes at all. The gentleman at the tax office, once he was over his astonishment, and had assured himself that I really wanted to do this insane thing (he himself would not have dreamed of it), fetched my file from the office next door, and having studied it, was lost in amazement.

'But,' he said, 'you have never deducted a penny from your income?'

'I had no idea I was entitled to,' I replied, at which he made anguished clucking sounds, drew up little columns of figures and then disappeared into another room with his calculations, returning eventually with a sheaf of little, but official looking pieces of paper.

'Now,' he said, 'we shall see what we can get back for you. We have the right to go back three years—only the last three years, *hélas*! But at least we can get you some money back for those three years. See, in fifteen days you will get a cheque for *this* amount. In another fifteen days a cheque for *this* amount. Then, at the last, a cheque for *this* amount.'

Three little pieces of paper, duly stamped, were handed over to me.

'For this current year, I think, we shall try to make you pay no taxes at all…'

'But, Monsieur—' I started.

'Durand,' he said. 'Felix Durand at your service.'

'I think, Monsieur Durand, that you have gone far enough ... I don't want you to get into trouble ... please, I prefer to pay this year's taxes ... I don't want any problems later on.'

'Problems!' exploded Felix Durand, 'Trouble! I am the *directeur* here ... If you have any problems, they will come to me! I shall see them off! I only wish we could go back further ... all that money wasted, gone off to the state...'

When I left his office on tiptoe, after fervently thanking him, he was still shuffling the papers in my file, murmuring sadly to himself, 'Three years ... only three years!'

A fortnight later, when I got the first cheque, it happened to be Valentine's day, so I sent Mr Durand a card to thank him. Promptly receiving a three-page letter in return, I thought it was not such a bad thing that I was leaving so soon. He was a sweet man, but hardly the stuff of my future, handy with the calculating machine as he might be.

Of course, I had been a fool to allow the accountant at my office fill my income tax forms for me (as I was the boss, and a woman to boot, not to mention a *young* woman, he probably had taken grim pleasure in making me pay the whole whack, year after year), but I was soon to be an even bigger one. After I'd been back in India for a while, a friend who was quite concerned about my old age (having visions perhaps of having to support me and Joshua herself) nagged me to find out about my pension from France. I did make enquiries, only to be told that I should have 'liquidated' my pension before leaving the country, and unless India and France could come to a mutual social-security arrangement, I unfortunately had no redress.

I wondered what Mr Durand would have made of that—it would have broken his heart—fifteen years of vast sums being deducted from my monthly salary, and none of that money back again? The folly! The sheer waste! As tragedy, it was at par with the worst—or the best—of Racine.

But back to our onions, as Mr Durand would say, as only the practical French can.

Double Trouble

ON A RAINY DAY DURING THE MONSOON SEASON, WHEN JOSH WAS just over a year old, Antonio had gone to the ophthalmologist to get his eyes checked. When he had returned the day before, Thomas had greeted him with such enthusiasm that his muzzle had crashed directly into Antonio's right eye and he had been seeing double after that.

I was just sponging Josh off (this happened about ten times a day during the rains) when I had to answer the front door. The little delivery boy from the grocery store was standing there, hopping from one leg to another like a stork.

'Amma,' he said, 'there's a dog outside you have to take!'

I replied that I had no intention of taking in another dog, but he was insistent.

I went out and saw a lean and hungry looking man on a rusty bicycle, with a villainous scythe strapped across the bar. On his dirty lap, he held a cocker spaniel who was the spitting image of Josh.

'When I saw him I thought,' said the boy, 'that he had stolen Joshua baba, so I stopped him on the road. Then when he didn't recognize me, I knew it was not Joshua baba. But it is a dog exactly like him, and where did that man get it from?'

Where indeed!

At the time, there was a flourishing trade in pedigreed dogs in a part of Russell Market. There were people who didn't want to pay the price the kennels were asking; there were rogues willing to help them. These entrepreneurs would go around secluded neighbourhoods, around the bungalows, taking photos of likely dogs in the gardens, keeping careful track of which dog belonged to which house. They would then create a photo album, which prospective buyers could consult. Once the buyer had selected a dog (and paid in advance, of course), the wretches would go out and steal it. Luckily, one of our neighbours had told me the whole story a while ago.

I asked the man if I could examine the dog. Up close, it was obvious that it was a girl and that she was at least two. Her resemblance to Joshua was nothing short of astonishing: every single marking tallied, except that the beauty spot she had on her right cheek was bigger than his. I asked the man what he was doing with her, and he gave me a long, involved (and certainly invented) story about why he was forced to sell her after having loved her for years.

I asked her name, and he replied, without a flicker of an eyelid—'Rani'. Of course, when I tried the name on her, the dog's eyelids didn't flicker either. It was obvious that she was much loved, and that she was used to trusting people. It was also clear that the villain had just stolen her, because she was spotless, her feathers neatly clipped, her coat brushed. Her family was probably crazed by her disappearance!

I called on our neighbour, Rustum, a great dog lover, who spoke Kannada (the local lingo) to negotiate the exorbitant asking price. Rustum finally bargained him down to a reasonable sum, helped by the fact that a heavy downpour had started, and the thief was anxious to get away from us and all our probing questions as quickly as possible.

I handed over the money, gave the dear boy from the grocery store a huge tip (it *could* have been Joshua, after all), and took Tess—for so I had named her, temporarily—inside to rub her down. She seemed quite at home with Josh and Tom and wasn't even hungry. In fact, she and Josh raced around the muddy garden and I had to hose them down and dry them twice over; I was pretty fed up by the time Antonio arrived.

I said nothing to him and let the 'twins' rush out to greet him, both in tearing spirits and barking their heads off. Poor Antonio obviously thought, at first sight, that his visit to the ophthalmologist had been in vain—he simply couldn't believe what he was seeing! Grounding himself in reality, he saw that there were *two* sets of barks, *two* bodies flinging themselves on him and *two* sets of teeth gripping his trousers. Of course, he was thrilled and moved instantly to action.

Laid on newspapers in the kitchen were now *two* bowls of milk, *two* bowls of chopped beef with vegetables, *two* bowls of cereal and *two* bowls of water. I could barely find place to manoeuvre and feed *myself*.

After half a day, we discovered that the only thing Tess would eat was bread and butter, so we gave it to her. She also pursued poor Joshua relentlessly. He got a taste, this time with a particular vengeance, of what it was like to be the one who was harassed, instead of the other way around. She simply wouldn't leave him alone, until Antonio roared at her on the second day, 'Lay off him, Tess … his balls haven't even dropped yet!'

In fact, that evening, when we went out to dinner with Edgar and Paulette down the road, we decided to take Tess with us and leave Josh to recuperate at home with a dog-sitter. Tess was delighted by the car ride and the company and behaved like a perfect lady. Our hosts, who had suffered from Joshua's rambunctious presence during many of their parties, were very grateful for the substitution and asked wistfully if we were planning on an exchange.

Naturally, we had called the SPCA and the Kennel Club as soon as we had invited Tess in, but we received no enquiries from her owners.

By the fourth day, Joshua was suffering from battle fatigue and he wasn't the only one. Having *two* cocker spaniels in bed with us made us walk around like zombies the next morning. Ours is an antique bed, and not really meant for two people, let alone four. Before he gave it to me in Paris, it had belonged to my friend Jean Daniel's Spanish great grandfather, and the people had all been shorter in those days.

Someone had obviously taught Tess to shake hands, which she did at the drop of a hat, but especially when she needed comfort or understanding.

That evening, Antonio was out at the opening of an exhibition and I was alone with the dogs. Unexpectedly, there was a dramatic thunderstorm—a window blew in with a crash, and the lights fused. This being Bangalore, they stayed fused while the wind blew eerily through the rain trees outside. Thomas, who was terrified of any loud noises, was huddled by my side. Every time I lit another candle, there was Tess, eyes spilling over with fear, offering me her big, soft paw. After three hours, my hand and her paw were both sore. I was tired and scared, and the candles had begun to run out, so I yelled at her, 'Oh, Tess, don't be such a bore!' She immediately yelped with fright, fell backwards over Josh—who also wanted to hold my hand—and ran to hide behind the sofa. I had to drag her out, apologise and offer biscuits all around in honour of her loyalty.

Anita came over the next morning with the local edition of the *Times of India* and triumphantly waved the Classified section in front of our noses. There was an ad for a lost cocker spaniel. The age, colour and size was indicated, explaining that she was under doctor's care, promising rich rewards and adding, with a touch of pathos, that her entire family was in mourning due to her disappearance. I called the number mentioned in the ad and put the lady who answered through a rigorous examination. She described Tess perfectly, told me she was just over two years old, had disappeared from their garden four days ago at 11 a.m. and that her name was Spotty.

I ask you, 'Spotty'—my, what a stupid name!

Anyway, I tried it on her—she perked up at once and barked. I told the lady she could come and collect her dog.

Fifteen minutes later, a tiny car drew up and disgorged an overweight young man, two overweight teenagers and an overweight matron with a mop of frizzy hennaed hair. Josh had, as usual, rushed out to greet the visitors with a stuffed alligator in his mouth. The matron—with a piercing shriek of 'My baby! My baby!'—snatched him up to her capacious bosom and started smothering him with kisses. I firmly disengaged him from her arms and told her that *her* baby was indoors. They all surged into the house to find Antonio lying on the sofa with Tess lying on top of him, both peacefully sharing a piece of buttered toast.

After the tears of reunion with their darling, I accepted reimbursement from the mother for what I'd paid for Tess. However, I urged them to go straight to Basha's grocery store and give the little delivery boy a huge reward for his foresight.

Tess came to visit us several times after that, and I eventually managed to persuade her mistress that Joshua was too young to be a father, even if his balls *had* dropped by now.

Putting on the Dog at the Dog Show

ON A QUIET, TREE-LINED STREET IN COOKE TOWN, MY FRIEND REVATHI, her husband SR and son Satish shared their bungalow with a shifting population of dogs. There was a core group of at least five which was regularly added to by Satish on his trips to visit dog breeders—they were all looked after by his patient parents, as he was too busy to follow-up on them. The in-house gang at the time I met them consisted of Mufassa, an enormous silver German Shepherd with icy blue eyes and a brain the size of a pea; Friskin, a portly dachshund who had a bowl of strong coffee at 5 a.m. and then spent his day playing football with tin lids, using his elbows; Timmy, a brindled mongrel; and Bruce and Chloe, prize-winning boxer dogs. Despite the fact that both Revathi and SR worked full-time, Revathi awoke at dawn to feed her dogs as well as to put out bowls to feed at least ten street mongrels twice a day.

Satish was much in demand throughout south India to show dogs at dog shows. So, when Joshua was almost two,

Satish pronounced him ready to make his professional debut, 'Although he is so spoiled, I shall have to come to your place to train him every evening to bring him up to the mark.' I wasn't in favour of the idea, but I'd never been to a dog show and was ready to give it a whirl. This met with the determined opposition of the concerned party, who was drilled every evening outside our house by Satish on how to stand, how to walk, how to run in the ring, not to mention the final, frozen pose for the judges.

After the first session, Satish was still optimistic; after a week, he came stamping into the house, dragging Josh (who had planted all four legs firmly on the ground throughout the session and refused to budge) and shouted, 'I've never, *ever*, seen such a stubborn and lazy animal in my life. He knows exactly what I want him to do—I know he understands every word—and he just does the exact opposite!'

Released, Josh put his paws on the coffee table, drained the flower bowl and lolled back against my knee, laughing into Satish's furious face. But Satish was adamant: go he would to the Kennel Club dog show the next Sunday.

Antonio was away on the big day—he was in Mumbai for the opening of his autumn show—so it was just Josh and myself, armed with brushes, water, lunch and cushions, who arrived at the Kennel Club at 8.30 a.m. The huge park was circled with little booths for each entry; each booth was provided with benches. Most of these benches were occupied by astonishingly well-behaved dogs, sitting to order like statues.

Josh gave these sissies an amazed, contemptuous look and dragged me at once on a round of the amusements. He greeted everyone, and everyone greeted him. We sampled some of the snacks on offer and made many new friends, but when we got back to our booth it was to the bad news that the working dogs would only be shown at 2 p.m.

By noon, Joshua, having spurned his lunch, was digging a hole in the booth halfway to China, sending up clouds of mud. His beautiful coat (that I had washed and brushed the day before) was a nice shade of brown, his nose was clotted with clay and he looked a sight. All around this demented figure, the experienced troupers continued sitting or lying on their benches as they had been trained to do.

I thought it was best to leave him be. By 2 p.m., he was moaning unhappily, and the sun was beating down like in the desert scene in *Lawrence of Arabia*. It was difficult to tell which of us was more fed up; we both longed for our shady bedroom and our regular siesta.

The punters and the merely curious were making the rounds. A portly gentleman approached our booth and asked me why Josh was in such a mess. 'He's missing his father,' I replied.

'Which kennel does he come from?'

'Well, at the moment, he's in Mumbai, having a show of his paintings.'

'My goodness!'

Finally, Satish came to fetch Josh. I hastily cleaned him up and begged him to be good. There were two adjoining rings and the cocker spaniel category would be evaluated by two judges, at intervals of an hour. The first round was being judged by an Australian. I couldn't bear to watch. Within half an hour Satish was back at our booth, puce-red in the face and perspiring heavily.

'I've never been so humiliated my whole life! He simply carted me around the ring at top speed and refused to stand still for one moment! He was only just placed, instead of getting the championship, as he should have. This bitch who didn't deserve it got it! Take him, take him away!'

He threw a leash and my panting dog at me and departed, speechless with anger.

Meanwhile, Revathi had entered Mufassa in the German Shepherd category—against Satish's orders—because she'd felt sorry for him; he had never been shown. He was summarily thrown out of the ring even before the class started, 'I'm judging dogs, not donkeys!' the judge had apparently said.

Poor Mufassa, who was, indeed, enormous, and who had compounded his lack of breeding in an attempt to put his paws on the judge's shoulders, was utterly downcast. So Revathi went and fetched a silver cup (which she had wisely brought along with her, all the way from home) and we rounded up about ten people to form a ring. Mufassa was then walked around the ring by Revathi; we all clapped madly and Muffay was handed the silver cup. He was thrilled to bits and did a victory lap to celebrate.

Satish had found a young boy whose father was showing dachshunds, and asked him to walk Josh for the second round; he said he couldn't face a second humiliation, his reputation had been besmirched enough. By now, the stuffing had gone out of even this hardiest of souls—poor Josh was utterly worn-out.

I told the boy his name, asked him to pet him, and they set off for the second ring. Following Satish's instructions, I crouched behind a car and watched through the windows. 'If he sees you, that'll be the end of it,' he had said.

In the event, I could see nothing because of the crowd. After what seemed like an interminable wait, the boy was back, flushed with triumph, with Josh trotting obediently to heel.

'He won, ma'am! He won all the prizes! The bitch who had won the first round snapped at the judge—he's the Nizam of Hyderabad after all, you know; he has hundreds of dogs, but he won't tolerate bad manners—he threw her out of the ring! Then Joshua walked perfectly; he ran with me and then, when we put him up on the table, he stood as quiet as a statue. Only thing is, he tried to kiss the Nizam, but the Nizam didn't mind because Josh didn't move. He got the Best of the Breed! And the best of opposite sex! Oh, ma'am, next week is the Ooty dog show—let me take him and show him there!'

I had absolutely no intention of taking Josh anywhere but home. Without waiting for the end of the show or the prize-giving ceremony, we took to our heels. The minute we got home, I bathed him, baked him a chocolate cake and we both sat in bed and ate it, getting crumbs in between the sheets liberally.

Revathi came proudly over the next morning, bearing Josh's cup and certificates. She was as mystified as I was as to what the title 'Best of Opposite Sex' meant, but the cup was very pretty. Josh also got a Kennel Club t-shirt. I put it on him, and he sat on the dining table with his trophies around him—waiting to welcome home his proud father.

Never again!

The Teddy Bears Picnic

WHEN ANTONIO RETURNED FROM HIS TRIP, HE HAD A SUITCASE FULL of doggie treats, including at least ten stuffed toys for Joshua—an entire menagerie of animals—which we referred to collectively as 'teddies'. The fact that Josh already had a whole shelf in the living room full of teddies had obviously been no deterrent to his besotted father.

For Thomas, that poor street boy who naturally had never had a toy and showed no interest in them, Antonio had brought a magnificent leash and chain and an assortment of flavoured bones, but only one teddy; a stuffed yellow shark. Josh got a blue one.

The minute Joshua—having subjected his new teds to a good examination—noticed Antonio handing the yellow shark to Thomas, he sprang to action. Thomas, who was looking down quizzically at his present, had it snatched from under his nose by this budding Othello, who then galloped to a corner of the room and tore it to pieces with great effort. He wasn't satisfied until it was in shreds, after which he looked over to Thomas triumphantly, as if to say, 'Now, what do you say to that?'

Thomas, to whom jealousy was a foreign emotion, just looked at this deluded soul sadly and turned his attention happily to his bones, which he knew were too solid for Josh to attempt to destroy.

We had friends called Debu and Nandita, whose Spitz, Bingo, was about three-years-old. He had faithfully invited Josh to all his birthday parties, a favour that Josh was in no hurry to return. The minute he saw Bingo (who was one of the most gentle and law-abiding dogs I have ever met) he would launch himself at his plumy tail and hang on with his razor sharp teeth, causing Bingo deep distress.

When Bingo next came to dinner with his parents, he immediately leapt up on the back of the sofa to avoid Josh's jaws. Unluckily, he was perched in a direction where his gaze was trained on the shelf crammed full with all of Josh's teddies. Noting his rapt attention our hero immediately sprang to attention. Darting looks of deep suspicion at the innocent Bingo (who had never had any stuffed toys himself and had never felt the lack, either), he collected, one by one, every teddy from the shelf to carry them to the other side of the room, creating a pile there. When he had safely corralled all his belongings, he sat on top of the pile—exhausted but satisfied—and gave Bingo a long and victorious look.

We had never seen such an exhibition of bad manners in our lives, but all our attempts to hand even the smallest teddy to Bingo (just as a lesson to Josh, not that our guest wanted it) brought forth volleys of furious barks from their rightful owner, who had absolutely no intention of sharing anything he owned.

I overreached myself one morning when, shopping at Commercial Street, I saw the most adorable (and enormous) toy basset hound for sale. It was disgracefully over-priced, but it also happened to be available in at least four other shop windows as I went down the street. Finally, I found one whose price was almost reasonable. I say almost, because when the shopkeeper, who was enquiring tenderly about how old my child was, discovered that I was buying a dog for a *dog*, almost refused to sell it to me, so outraged was he. His baser instincts won, but he was still sadly shaking his head at this queer customer when I walked out with my offering of love.

When we moved to Goa in 2000, I laundered all of Josh's teddies and packed them into two large cartons. However, from his first view of the enormous new garden in the house we had rented, the fishpond, and above all, his first experience of the sea, Josh lost all interest in the toys of his youth. As it was nearing Christmas, I then decided to let every child visiting us thereafter choose a teddy as a present. But I should have known Josh better. He may no longer have wanted all of them around, but they were *his*.

His first victim was Adele, a four-year-old cousin of ours, who chose a large green frog and ran happily to display it to her parents in the sitting room. When Josh realized exactly what she was brandishing, such was his haste to retrieve it that he skidded on his bottom over to her and tore it out of her hand. They then had a merry chase around the house for more than an hour, snatching the frog from one another, until Adele was red in the face and Josh panting like a steam engine.

After that incident, I would usually take the chosen child into the bedroom, lock the door behind me, let the child make their choice and then put the teddy in a plastic bag, which I would then hand over to the child only when the visitors were safely in their car and on the verge of leaving (Josh has a keen sense of smell—after all, he was bred to be a gun dog).

The only casualty was the enormous basset hound, because two little girls, also young cousins who were sisters, both wanted it. Annika and Anya's wails as they grabbed it from each other drew everyone to the bedroom, including Josh, who leapt into the fray with the light of battle in his eyes. The trio were finally parted, and the basset put in a large bag (Josh having been coaxed to unclench his jaws by a large piece of cake waved under his nose) and my cousins all went home rather quickly.

I was not popular with their mother Sonali after that, as she told me that the battle between her daughters had continued in the plane all the way back to their home in Pune. She said that after they had gotten back, she had been forced to confiscate the hound and give it to the first visitor she had (this person was leaving town). Neither of her daughters was speaking to her.

So, we leave behind childhood, although Josh, ever a creature of habit, expects us to bring him back a teddy every time either of us leaves home for any length of time. We now confine ourselves to getting the smallest variety.

It is, of course, understood that Antonio and I never leave home at the same time—Joshua would never stand for that. One or any of our friends would have been proud and happy to give Thomas house room if ever he had need of it, but none of them have the time, the constitution or the sheer nerve to take Joshua on.

When I had to leave him for the first time to go to Lavinia's wedding in Paris, I was standing in the aircraft in the tiny space reserved for us depraved smokers—holding a bidi in one hand and an album of photos in the other—and having a good cry. The Frenchman next to me patted me gently on the shoulder and asked solicitously if I were missing my man. 'No,' I sobbed, 'my little boy—look at him, how beautiful he is!'

I have to say that none of my friends in Paris—who were eagerly awaiting photos of Antonio, of Bangalore, of our friends and of our home there—showed any enthusiasm at being presented with sheaves and sheaves of Joshua's photos in every possible attitude and at every possible age—from the blob of babyhood to the long-eared, dewy-eyed, leggy beauty of nearly a year old. 'Yes, yes, very nice,' they would say perfunctorily, 'we know all about him already' and return to desperately turning over the photos to try to find something other than this canine marvel.

But they searched in vain.

The Land of Sun, Sea ... and Zachariah

WHEN JOSHUA WAS TWO, WE DECIDED TO MOVE TO GOA BECAUSE OF the increasing pollution in Bangalore. Real estate was booming in this 'happening' town, and all around us, old bungalows were being demolished in preparation for the construction of apartment buildings in their stead. We knew it was time to head for greener pastures before things got worse.

Goa, at that point in time, had not yet become the *Côte d'Azur* of India. Nor was it yet the place where the rich from the metropolises built their second homes. However, it was a favourite holiday destination; we had many contacts there, not to mention family, and it was still possible to rent a pretty large house with a garden in one of the villages.

Viki, Josh's godfather, lent us his jeep and driver for the trip to Goa and we set off at 4 a.m. with all the street turning out to say goodbye to us, as well as Revathi and her family. Two of my street mongrel friends, Badger and Scholastica, watching our furniture leave in a truck with apprehension, had simply moved in the night before and slept on the floor with us. SR had to put them in his car and drive them back to the park before we left. It was very sad to say goodbye to the companions of our morning walks.

We were driving down because there was no way Josh would have let himself be crated in a train or a plane. Because of him, we had a twelve-hour journey ahead of us instead of a two-hour one. Thomas had never before been in a car for a long trip. He sat on a rug in the back of the jeep—rigid with fear but totally trusting—and never moved a whisker during the entire journey. His happiness that he was going with us overrode his apprehension. Not so his younger brother, who'd been taking car rides since he was three weeks old.

This car ride never stopped! The 'good' place where he could eat, drink and then go home never seemed to arrive. Despite the sedative we had given him, he vocalised his disappointment during the entire trip, like Maria Callas in the last act of *Madame Butterfly*, occasionally giving us excerpts from the mad scene in *Lucia*. He refused to settle down, barked incessantly and bounded from one window to the other. Antonio and I took turns, sitting with this monster in the back seat, switching every three hours. By nightfall (always early in India), he was exhausted but unbowed. He kept shaking his head to stay awake, still determined not to succumb to sleep. By the time we arrived at the house we had rented in a village in north Goa, we were limp with fatigue.

Nevertheless, it was a marvellous place for the boys, with a series of three gardens and a river at the bottom of the last one where we could collect mussels in season. It was hotter than it had been in Bangalore, but the scenery was ravishing: unlike the northern beach strip, the inland villages of Goa were as yet mostly unspoiled. The whole state was laced with rivers and half of it stretched alongside the Arabian Sea—a coastline fringed by sandy beaches, coconut palms and forested hills. The age of plastic and the bulldozer had not yet arrived in force to change the beauty of the greenery of Goa, nor to pollute its rivers, and we were to enjoy this bounty for ten full years.

Josh's first taste of the seaside was an epiphany for him. Cocker spaniels are water dogs; he was in his element. From the moment we arrived at the beach and for the following three hours—at the end of which we forced him to come home with us—he was delirious with joy. He chased the seagulls from the dunes into the sea, plunged after them into the waves and then chased them back into the dunes, all the while barking at the top of his voice. He was in heaven!

Thomas, who never got over his distrust of the sea, stayed at a safe distance, indulging in his favourite pastime. He would find a bush or a long clump of feathery grasses and put his head into it. He would then commence to slowly revolve his back legs, in what Antonio called 'Thomas' tai chi'. It was his way of centring himself after each new and startling experience, not to mention a complete change of lifestyle. He became known as the 'Zen Buddhist', which suited him very well, especially as he had to cope with Joshua as a fellow voyager.

However, even Thomas was unable to cope with an event that overtook us.

The monsoon had broken, bringing a welcome end to the unbearable heat. Our maid Sushila's husband came to us one morning, holding out his hand. On it was a miniscule puppy, practically a new-born. What we could see through the mud was a pure white coat and a pair of light blue eyes. He said that he had found it on his way to work lying by the highway alone in a puddle of rainwater and couldn't bear to leave it there. Of course, we Good Samaritans had to help this orphan.

Christening him Zachariah, Antonio and I fed the tiny scrap with a medicine dropper every two hours. We took turns feeding him at night, sleeping in the guest room with him and an alarm clock. He was rocked to sleep, sung to and pampered, all under the glassy eye of Joshua, who had absolutely no desire to be upstaged and who took to jumping onto the swing—where I held Zach in my lap—and trying to sit on him in a vain attempt to make him disappear.

Zach grew rapidly, and it was very soon clear that he was not going to be a beauty. My sister Sunita, a clinical psychologist, claims that this was the point at which I lost interest in him and that the rest of Zach's career was an effort to win back my attention by being as wicked as he possibly could.

Be that as it may, his white coat quickly turned the colour of old teeth; his eyes changed colour and became small, close-set and brown; he seemed possessed by an evil spirit.

In order to let the boys eat in peace, Zach was fed in the kitchen while the other two were fed in the veranda. However, Zach would bolt his food without even tasting it and then rush out to push Thomas and Josh away from their bowls. He would knock down pretty little Sushila in the kitchen if she had a bowl of food in her hand, gobble the contents from the floor and then be sick.

He was soon jumping over the garden wall and ranging farther afield for his pleasures. Typically, he preferred attacking little children and old people. Antonio tried to explain away Zachariah's violent ways by saying that they stemmed from 'the trauma of his birth and abandonment' and that, with continued loving care, he would eventually learn to trust the outside world. However, it was not just the outside world but also we who had to bear the fallout.

We were going to move house after a year. I tried to reason with Antonio. Sushila and her husband were not moving with us. However, they felt a sense of responsibility for introducing this demon into our home and were prepared to keep him—rather, let him run loose in their neighbourhood, which had lots of dogs. They begged us to leave this budding Genghis Khan with them and not take him with us.

Antonio wavered. One day he would agree to my pleas; the next day he would change his mind, unwilling to abandon an orphan. In all this, he was strongly supported by my brother-in-law, Arjun, who was even worse than Antonio—if such a thing is possible—as far as tenderness towards animals was concerned. Sunita said that if they had had a house and garden instead of an apartment, their two beagles, Benjamin and Franklin, would be sharing the bed with Arjun, and she would have to make do with the kennel. If she called out for a blanket, she said, Arjun would have told her to lower her voice because she was disturbing the dogs' sleep. While this was an exaggeration, it wasn't so by much—Antonio and Arjun were united in their folly.

At the very last minute, Antonio reneged on his promise yet again and Zachariah moved with us to our new villa. This was in a village quite close by, set in flat fields that were much lower than the surface of the roads. This gave Zachariah (who by now was leaping the five-foot garden wall in the new house) splendid opportunities to attack the helpless villagers on the road, who then fell into the paddy fields below. He also—and this was a truly frightening development—started chasing cows. Everyone knows the importance of cows in

India and the penalties for damaging them, and this village moreover had a primarily Hindu population. The situation was getting critical.

At this juncture, Antonio went to Toronto for a month. His departure had a terrible effect on Zachariah, making him totally anti-social, as if Antonio had been the only person who had kept alive some tiny, remaining spark of decency in him and diluted his apparent hatred of the entire world.

It made one consider the question of evil. Apparently, just as some people, irrespective of having had every advantage, like loving families and good education, turn out to be simply *bad*, so do animals. No matter what my sister said, there was simply no other explanation for Zachariah's bloodlust towards all and sundry (Antonio not excepted). He was by now more than a year old and it was only too obvious that nothing was going to change him. He would only become *more* himself, so to speak. Thomas and Joshua gave him a wide berth—their only desire was to stay as far away from him as possible.

With Antonio's departure, the boys and I—not to mention a series of maids, all of whom gradually deserted us because of Zachariah—were at his mercy. By now, such was his ferocity that I was forced to lock him up on the veranda and lower his food to him through the window in the sitting room. The rest of us used the back door of the villa, and we had to warn any guests who were planning to visit us to avoid the front entrance and to come to the back garden to meet us.

The last straw was the evening I decided to give him one last chance and after having fed him a huge meal, let him into the house. He sat ominously still for about ten minutes and then, with no provocation whatsoever, leapt at my throat. Luckily, I managed to raise my arm in time to fend him off, but darling Joshua, like the brave Lochinvar, immediately charged to my rescue. In a lightening move, Zach whisked around and sank his teeth into Joshua's flank.

That was it! There could be no possible future for us together now. Although I had tried to find another 'home' for him (whatever *home* meant to this animal), I had had no success. There was no question of giving a savage dog to anyone I knew, and all the animal shelters had already refused to 'shelter' him. I had to take the situation in hand before something awful happened to us or anyone else. I thought about it for a good, long time and hit on what seemed to me to be the only solution. I resolved to say nothing to anybody about what I had decided to do and laid my plans accordingly.

The very next day, I called for a taxi in the morning. Having fed—or rather, thrown—Zach a substantial meal through the window, I put on a thick raincoat and gardening gloves to protect myself. I filled a box with biscuits, let myself out onto the veranda and lured Zach down the garden path and into the taxi by laying a trail of biscuits. I slammed the door behind us and screwed my courage to the sticking point.

The cab driver must have thought I was crazy, but I just told him to drive as quickly as he could, as far as he could, in any direction away from the village and the main highway. I said I would tell him when to stop. The only time I could tell him when to stop would be when I ran out of biscuits, which I was doling out to Zachariah at regular intervals. Naturally, I kept my eyes on the floor, because I didn't want to have the faintest idea of where we were going. I knew only too well that I would be extensively grilled by Antonio when he returned, and I wanted to deny any knowledge of our final destination with a clear conscience.

Finally, after a roller-coaster ride—the cab driver had taken me seriously, apart from also not being at all reassured by the snarls he was hearing from the back seat—I reached the penultimate biscuit.

'Stop!' I shouted to the driver, and the cab screeched to a halt at once. I threw open the door and simultaneously flung out the last biscuit. Zachariah shot out of the door in pursuit, caught the biscuit in mid-air and flew into a thicket of trees and flowering creepers without a backward look at me.

I slammed the door shut and shouted 'Go, go!' urgently. The cab shot forward. It soon reached a dead-end and had to backtrack. It couldn't have been more than a couple of minutes before we got back to the fatal spot, but there was no sign whatsoever of Zachariah. I imagined how Josh or Thomas would have behaved if ever—of course, that would be *never*—I had abandoned them in a strange place. They would have waited forever for me to come back. Not so Zachariah. He had already made it so obvious that he didn't feel a thing for us.

I was so overwrought and drained by the whole experience—not to mention the whole past year with Zachariah—that I simply fell to the floor of the cab and started babbling Ave Marias in thanksgiving. I couldn't care less about what the cab driver was thinking—he undoubtedly thought I was a lunatic, but I had promised him triple his normal fare and he wasn't going to complain.

I got home, told the cab to wait, tore off my clothes, changed and told the maid to disinfect the entire house. Then I went to the beauty parlour—I hadn't enjoyed such a luxurious, dreamless hour for a very, very long time.

After the beauty parlour, I went shopping. I bought bags of freshly made tandoori chicken, an assortment of naan rotis, spiced mutton chops and a huge tub of lychee ice-cream.

When I got back, a heavenly peace seemed to have descended over the house. All the doors and windows were open; everything smelt fresh and clean; Josh and Thomas were romping in the sun in the front garden. The birds were singing in the honeysuckle hedge and so was my heart; it was warbling away as I joined my boys on the grass and romped with them. That evening, we danced, all three of us; we lay around on the carpet; we ate all the wonderful food. In fact, we had a love feast. All of us went to bed and slept peacefully and for long. The evil spell had been broken. The devil had departed. We had been delivered.

My sister Sunita, with her lurid imagination, described Zach's future to us. As he was the only 'real' Goan among all of us, having been born and lived only in Goa, she re-named him 'Maniac Fernandes' (anyone who has heard of footballers in Goa named Climax, or doctors named Maverick, will not be surprised). By now, she says, he will have collected a large gang of bad boys; they will roam the countryside, wreaking havoc. Maniac Fernandes, as leader, wears a red bandana round his neck, and remains in the van of the attack as well as of the retreat. He lives alone in a room, which is plastered with photos of myself, all with large black crosses defacing my visage. One day he, as leader of the gang of Kill Kill Boys will be apprehended and sentenced to death. In his little room, he will have exchanged his red bandana for a black one and scrawled 'It's all your fault' across the photos.

Outside, Antonio and Arjun, who have appealed for a stay of the death sentence, will be keeping a candlelight vigil and praying for a last-minute reprieve. Their prayers will not be answered, and it will all be because of me.

No Sex Please, I'm Joshua

JOSHUA WAS NOW THREE, AND IT WAS TIME HE BECAME A MAN. REVATHI had explained to me that, for the sake of his health, he had to be mated at least once a year.

My mother had not relished the moment when I had pushed Josh towards her and said, 'Go and give your grandmother a great, big kiss.'

However, he was the only grandson she was likely to get from me, and she made the best of it as she was a deeply sensible woman. Also, she already had six grandchildren from her other three children, and I had always swum against the tide. She went with the flow. Josh loved going to her house, where he got all the deep-fried snacks that Goa is famous for, which he never got at home. She, in the process of writing her fourth cookbook, was always happy to meet a good eater who wasn't afraid to experiment. She eventually forgot herself enough to actually say 'Come to Grandma' when they met, at which he would fling himself on her and smother her with excited kisses.

Thomas, before he adopted us, had been castrated by CUPA ('Caring Unlimited, Positive Action', an animal organization in Bangalore that our friend Sheila Rao had helped to start and which had a splendid programme for sterilizing street dogs), so he didn't have much choice as far as the opposite sex was concerned.

It was up to Joshua to people our family tree. However, during the mating seasons, he had never shown any interest when all the other male dogs had been baying to the moon and keeping the entire neighbourhood awake. In fact, he had never shown the slightest interest, apart from Thomas, in anything on four legs, be it male or female. Two-leggeds were a different story. Josh had a keen appreciation for pretty women. When a beauty called Amber came over one evening, her charms shown off in a low-cut red velvet dress, Joshua simply jumped onto her lap, closed his eyes in thankfulness at his good fortune, pushed his head gently down into her perfumed *décolleté* and refused to budge. Amber had at least three dogs of her own and was suitably touched by this heartfelt homage.

Josh had a particular way while communicating deeply with me—he'd raise his head slowly till his nose was pointing at the sky, and with eyes closed, he would let his chest swell in emotion. I called it 'the butterfly stretch', and he would do it for me whenever I got him in the right mood. I later saw my sister's beagle, Benjy, doing the same thing to her. She explained to me that, in dog parlance, it meant 'I love you'.

Nevertheless, I was concerned for his health, and there was no lack of suitable girls in Goa to satisfy the desires of even the most exacting lover. I put an ad in the papers (suitable girl of good family wanted for beautiful and friendly cocker spaniel, no stud fee), with a photo of Joshua attached to the ad. Besides the newspaper, I put the ad up in our local supermarket. Everyone thought the whole thing was very funny, except Josh and myself. We were very proud of the photo, which showed him in all his splendour—chin up, soulful profile showing, posing in front of one of Antonio's more colourful canvases.

We then became hosts to a succession of hopeful brides. First, there was Twinkle, a massive, stolid black cocker, who patiently and continuously offered her rear end to Josh, while he, after a first, courteous sniff at it, went about his normal routine. She was a heavy eater and didn't have much personality.

Then there was Mia, a blue-roan, who had a passion for water. The minute she spotted the fish pond in the garden, she immediately made a beeline for it and dived in. As it was very shallow, she was quite safe, but after the tenth rescue operation (she simply jumped in and sank like a stone—alas, not very bright) we had to call her parents and ask them to take her home because she seemed more interested in becoming a mermaid than a mother.

Elsa came next, a rangy, twitchy and extremely neurotic chestnut beauty. She needed the couch rather than a mate, because she would have driven any suitor crazy. She would leap on Joshua and get him all worked up and then, when he attempted to get to know her better, she would screech in alarm and shoot off, ending up in Antonio's arms, wailing for help. She also couldn't do with anyone but Antonio in bed with her, so Josh and I moved into the spare room.

In case you're wondering, Thomas always had a splendid sofa to himself, and was quite happy in the sitting room, as he needed his space for his Zen meditation.

Elsa's mother was summoned and she departed, wailing for Antonio, who was her idea of a demon lover.

Finally, Honey arrived. She was indeed the colour of her name, and for the first time, Joshua fell in love. She was inexperienced and he was inept, much as I hate to have to say this. Between them, as they grappled with each other in vain, they kept us in a constant state of anxiety. On top of this, Honey's family refused to let her *découcher*. In France, it is considered very bad form to spend the whole night in your lover's house. Do whatever you want to do, but be in your own bed when breakfast time arrives. Honey's family obviously had the strictest ideas about what was what.

As the pair obviously didn't seem to be able to manage the mating on their own, after three days we called on professional help. The dog handler told us that usually the girl was brought to the boy's home, as the male generally could not perform with any confidence unless he was on his home turf. We assured him that, if there was anything that Joshua lacked, it wasn't self-confidence. So, the two families left in convoy for the dog handler's home, with the lovesick pair moaning to each other out of their respective car windows.

The dog handler seemed to know his business, but when it reached the critical moment, I couldn't watch. Honey's mother and I fled into the woods while the deed was done. For once in his amorous dog life, Joshua performed with panache, but alas, there was no '*suite*': no follow up, as the French say.

Either Honey couldn't conceive or her period of fertility was over. Or, as Arjun said brutally, as he was preparing to bring Benjy and Franky to Goa on holiday, 'I'm going to take you to meet your gay cousins.' My dearest friend in India, Sarojini, was kinder to everyone. 'Why,' she said in her gentle, caressing voice, 'would he want anyone else? He thinks you're his wife.'

After this, we gave up, as Joshua clearly didn't have much stomach for the enterprise and, in any case, he *had* succeeded with Honey, even if no puppies had blessed their union. One desperate owner of a strawberry blonde female cocker suggested artificial insemination, but this was clearly in the realm of the absurd, and Joshua, whatever he lacked in the sex department, had great dignity and a horror of making a fool of himself. He had never had that painful habit of humping people's knees or legs which one finds so distasteful in more abandoned—or desperate—dogs. If he did make a fool of himself, it was in a spectacular fashion.

At this point, Antonio and I, far from spending each minute with our boys, were in fact working very hard. Antonio had several shows lined up in Mumbai or Delhi, and they all came with deadlines; I had thrown myself, with a passion that alarmed him, into painting in acrylic full-time. After all the encouragement that Antonio had given me over the years to start painting, I was so inspired by the lushness of Goa that I dived right in, and instead of resisting his efforts to make me paint, it now seemed that he'd created a Frankenstein. After a little more than a year, I was lucky enough to have a solo show of my paintings in a gallery in Mumbai, after which I confined myself to group shows.

One of these was held in Goa as part of a festival of the arts, showcased in the older part of Mapusa. Mapusa was the market town close to us, and despite the wholesale (and ugly) development that had wrecked its original charm, the oldest part of the town and the crowning feature of the hill had managed to retain a collection of beautiful old heritage homes, some of them empty.

For the duration of the three-day festival, the owners of most of these houses had kindly allowed the artists to show their work in their homes, in a balcony or a large room or even, in the cases of the unoccupied houses, the entire space.

In the evenings, a wide variety of food stalls in the streets and parks of that area were set up, to sell traditional sweets and savouries; there were also traditional games and an open-air orchestra. For the first two days of the festival, I left the boys at home with the maid.

On the third and last day, Alexis, the well-known Goan cartoonist, had organized the first ever public English poetry reading in Goa, at around 7 p.m., in one of the most beautiful colonial family homes within the festival space. He had asked me to introduce the event and to read some of my poetry. I decided to take Joshua with me to join in the fun and leave him in charge of two of my fellow artists, Sonatina and Charmaine, who were both showing their work at the same house as I was.

I set off with Josh, armed with a freshly baked strawberry shortcake, oatmeal biscuits and a quiche. I figured that this assortment would keep him happy for at least an hour, while the reading would take place and that he would be thrilled by the company. Joshua had always been partial to pretty girls, and these two were real peaches.

I had actually seen him, on many toe-curling occasions, refuse to say hello to a woman who wasn't up to his standards of feminine beauty.

I sneaked away quietly from the place we were showing, a little before seven, noting that Josh was fully occupied with his court—I walked leisurely up to the venue, stopping to chat with friends on the way.

The room the reading was to take place in was the central hall of the house, and it was packed with at least sixty or seventy people, which immediately gave me cold feet. I simply couldn't stand up and emote in front of so many people, so I was allowed to sit with Alexis; with a large and potted palm tree partially screening my face, in front of the audience.

I gave my introduction and, as I was still too nervous to start the reading, asked Victor Rangel Ribeiro, a reputed Goan writer and a dapper gentleman of over eighty, to read first. Victor explained that he had only written one poem in his life, which had been the deciding factor that had persuaded his wife to marry him and that, thrilled by his good luck, he'd never dared to write another one. He then read a charming poem written by a friend of his in New York, about re-visiting his ancestral home in Goa. A very emotional lady, who obviously had been through a bad patch in her life, followed him.

Then came a tall, upstanding fellow, hung with gold chains and carrying an ominously tall sheaf of papers (each of the poets had been allocated not more than five minutes each, as there seemed to be a surprising number of them). This bravo announced that he was going to read from an unpublished—deservedly, as it turned out—collection of his father's poems, called *Gypsies of the Sea* and in a booming voice started to trace the life of the fishermen of Goa practically back to their sea bed, growing increasingly lost in the mists of antiquity. After ten minutes of tortured blank verse, the audience began to fidget. After fifteen, my legs began to cramp and fearful of what would follow this performance, I whispered to Alexis that I wanted to go next. Alexis managed to persuade the chap to break-off mid-verse, right when the fishermen had barely embarked on their early morning catch, and I then read (while still sitting) the three poems I had brought with me.

As I finished the third one, there was an ear-splitting, crashing noise in the veranda, and the door to the hall flew open. Joshua burst into the room, ears flying, barking in a crazed manner, with Sonatina practically airborne at the end of his leash. She had to let go, at which point Joshua galloped towards me, upending several chairs and their occupants on the way. He leapt at me, and my chair fell over backwards. I was laid out on the floor and he had landed safely on my chest with a resounding thump. The breath had been knocked out of me, but I was only thankful that I was wearing, for once, a long skirt—not to mention underwear.

Josh continued to sit on me, panting happily, covering my face with relieved kisses. Most of the audience knew (and cordially disapproved of) Joshua and were probably dying to apply the palms of their hands to his butt, but they restrained themselves for my sake and eventually order was restored. I picked Josh up, checked that I had no limbs broken, and quietly tiptoed out the back way. Victor told me later that the event had gone steadily downhill from then on, poetry-wise, and that I'd been lucky that Josh had arrived on the scene to rescue me. Sonatina, as mortified as I was, explained that once Joshua had realized I was gone, there was absolutely no way of making him stay put. He woke echoes with his barking and simply insisted on following my trail; she had had no choice in the matter.

However, from then on, I tried my poetry out on Josh, and I have to say that he was a most discriminating audience, as long as there were only the two of us. Naturally, he preferred my work over that of far better poets. I had, at that time, a passion for Garcia Lorca and every time he would hear me begin, on an emotional note, 'I want to sleep the dream of the apples' he would sigh, put his head on my knee and compose himself for a long nap.

One of my cousins, a confirmed dog-hater, was the only one who stood up to Joshua. Of course, he knew in advance what to expect—all of our families and friends had been entirely vocal on the subject. The first time he visited us in Goa, Joshua, as usual, tore out of the house at the sound of a stranger's voice, barking loudly and preparing to launch himself in welcome. My cousin Kit thundered, 'Be quiet, Joshua!' Josh was so astounded that he stopped mid-leap and landed with a thump—on his bottom. Nobody had ever, ever, spoken to him in that tone of voice before! He didn't open his mouth once throughout the entire evening, but retreated to a corner of the room and sat there in silence, agog with astonishment at this new species that didn't seem to appreciate him, and moreover, didn't even seem to notice his existence, except to glare at him at regular intervals.

'So,' said Kit as he left, 'D'you want me to drop in everyday and give him another dose? I guarantee I'll have him perfectly behaved in under a week!'

Different People, Different Animals

OF COURSE, I OFTEN THOUGHT OF MY LIFE IN FRANCE, AND WISHED I were at a table shaded by a chestnut tree, drinking *beaujolais nouveau* and savouring a duck *pâté* with a *salad caprice des années folles* with my old friends who had been such a major part of my life. But only as long as Josh was at my side too, of course.

If you looked at the railway map of France, kept behind glass in every train compartment in that country, you would see that the end of the line in the southeast was a town called Quillan. It was in the Oriental Pyrennes, very close to Andorra and the Spanish border. To get to Quillan, in this rugged and mountainous area, one took a smaller branch of the regular railway line from the beautiful walled town of Carcassonne. The track ran through tiny villages perched precariously on the mountain slopes, alongside a pebbly trout river called the Aude.

I had the good fortune to have discovered—or rather, they claim they discovered me—French 'cousins'. The exact line of parentage is unclear; we all now acknowledge that the ancestral blood is far from direct, but what is indisputable is that their grandfather was Indian, of Goan extraction, and that he shared the same family name, Heredia, with my maternal grandmother, Emilia.

From the surviving photographs of him, we learn that this gentleman was over six feet tall, with a dashing moustache, and family legend has it that he was a poet. He had crossed the ocean from Goa to France, married a diminutive French lady who played the piano and sired a single son. Very romantically, they lived a little out of Quillan, on an island. The island was not large, but the house on it was perfectly situated: successively ringed by flowery meadows, a belt of woodland, a tributary of the river Aude, and finally, by the mountains which remained snow-capped even in the summer.

When he was still only in his thirties, José Maria de Heredia (for so he styled himself, which occasioned some pleasurable confusion with the French poet of the same name) embarked on a voyage back to Goa to settle some family business. Sadly, he fell ill during the voyage, died and was buried at sea. Neither his wife nor his son ever visited India, but his four grandchildren took a lively interest in this country of their heritage.

The first of them to visit India, François Xavier, crossed paths with me on my way to Paris in 1976. When he came back to France, having visited most of our shared extended family in India, he came to see me at Catherine's house and took me to meet the rest of the grandchildren, who in turn took me to their collective bosom. In descending order, they were Marie José, José Maria, François Xavier and Gérald. At that point in time, only José Maria was married, and he and his wife Agnès had just had their first child, Alexandra.

Over the years, we made many trips together to 'l'Ile', as the house on the island was called. Their widowed mother, Jacqueline, lived there by herself all the year round, busy with her rose and vegetable gardens, her rabbits and other livestock. She kept a breed of dogs called schnauzers, who were barred from entering the house, although the princely German Shepherd, Igor, was occasionally allowed inside as a treat.

The first time I went to l'Ile, one of the schnauzers, called Jenny, took an instant dislike to me. No sooner had we gotten out of the car than, without a warning, she came at me from behind and bit me on the seat of my trousers. Marie José and Gérald, who were with me, were horrified, but Jacqueline, who had just come out to greet us, clasped her hands in ecstasy and then crossed herself (she was very devout) exclaiming, 'At last! At last I have a proper guard dog!'

About ten years later, when she had decided to keep only one dog at a time, she bought a giant schnauzer, coal black in colour. As the Kennel Club rule in France was to name each pedigreed dog according to the letter of the alphabet for that year, Jacqueline named her puppy Tanya, for the year of the letter T. I, of course, was madly flattered but her children all thought it was a great insult. None of them were dog lovers, so there was no reason for them to understand that I regarded it a compliment.

Alas—or *hélas*, as the French would say—Tanya turned out to be a complete slob, and a gigantic clumsy slob at that. She was extremely affectionate, but also completely boneheaded. The cousins would wince every time they heard Jacqueline call out, 'Tanya, you wicked—' or stupid, or dirty, or disobedient

'—girl, look at the mud on the floor!' or the overturned table, or the digging in the garden or any of a thousand, daily crimes committed by my vigorous namesake, who simply couldn't contain her boundless energy.

Finally, Jacqueline was rewarded by Isora, who was not only a terrific watchdog, but also gentle as a lamb with the family. Isora and I spent happy hours together on the terrace. I would sit with a book on the sun-warmed steps, flanked by huge stone pots of brightly-coloured geraniums—fuchsia, cerise and magenta—and Isora would sit behind me, with her head on my shoulder, contentedly gnawing at my plaited hair.

Jacqueline adopted a very pragmatic attitude towards her animals. Dogs were kept, fed and walked in return for guarding the house, cats for catching mice and rabbits bred for the stew-pot or the market. I was particularly fond of a large, dove-coloured female rabbit called Angélique but Jacqueline did not share my feelings. According to her, Angélique was not worth her cabbage leaves, as she had stubbornly failed to reproduce. 'She refuses the male,' was Jacqueline's running refrain. In other words, she was not earning her keep and her time was running out.

One summer weekend, when Marie José and I arrived at l'Ile from Paris, both of us famished, Jacqueline greeted us with a steaming casserole of rabbit *ragoût*. She was, anyway, a marvellous cook, and I had at least three helpings. Jacqueline watched me wipe my plate clean with the good, crusty bread of the Pyrennes with a fond smile.

'Was it good?'

'It was divine,' I replied.

'Good, good, I am so glad you enjoyed it. You were so fond of Angélique that I saved her specially for you to enjoy.'

This attitude was the direct opposite of my dear friend Lavinia's approach to animals. *Mi casa es su casa*, as the Spanish saying goes—my house is your house—was never truer than in her case where animals were concerned. We had met in the back row of a classroom at the Sorbonne, both ostensibly there to take a degree in the French language. The degree, on my part, was achieved with the greatest difficulty ('You see before you a desperate case,' had said our teacher Mademoiselle Dianne, raising an accusing finger in my direction while I waited, knees knocking, to take the oral exam in front of a board of examiners), but our friendship had nevertheless progressed, in inverse proportion to my mastery of the French language.

Lavinia, a perfect *quattrocento* beauty, was Italian but had been brought up in the US, where she returned after two years of studying art history in Europe. Eventually, after having visited me regularly, she moved to Paris. At one point in time, she lived in a roomy, airy apartment with parquet flooring on the third floor of an apartment building overlooking the *Père Lachaise* cemetery gardens. She never had time to feel lonely, as her roommates were her cat Bunny, whom she had adopted as a kitten from the SPCA in Chicago and brought to Paris when she moved there; a little stray mongrel called Cocoloco whom she had rescued in the street while on holiday in Madrid because he was injured; a pet dwarf rabbit called Ducon; and Daffodil, a baby pigeon that had fallen from a tree in front of my house when she had come to dinner.

All of them had the run of the house: Coco limping in his Elizabethan collar because of his damaged leg; Ducon merrily bounding after him; Daffodil waddling around because he had no intention of learning how to fly; and Bunny, safely perched on a radiator, watching the menagerie with a jaundiced eye.

'Who,' said Lavinia's mother Luciana, when she visited from her home in Italy, 'is going to marry you, my poor child? You're living in a zoo!'

A good home was found for Cocoloco on a farm in the south of Italy; he eventually became the leader of the pack there. Bunny was a fixture, but Daffodil and Ducon were another matter: Daffodil, having been reared literally on Lavinia's soft bosom, hand-fed and sung to in Schubert's *leider*, had never had it so good. Finally, when he was almost a year old, I persuaded Lav that it was time he joined his brethren. Besides, I had a phobia of birds: there was that morning when I opened her kitchen door, having forgotten that he was closed in there—our mutual fright when I started screaming was not an experience either of us wanted to repeat.

So, Lavinia followed my advice and took Daffodil to the *Père Lachaise* gardens below, which were naturally full of pigeons. Three hours later, she called me at my office in great excitement.

'So, how did it go?'

'Well, I stayed there for three whole hours! It was great!'

'What did you do?'

'I sat on a bench and read.'

'But where was Daffodil?'

'At my feet … he was so good; he didn't budge all the time!'

'No, Lav, you have to leave him by the bench and go sit far away. That's the whole point—he has to meet his brothers and sisters.'

So, the next day, Lavinia hardened her heart and did just that. After an hour, she could bear it no longer and rushed back to the spot she'd left him at. Naturally, there were masses of pigeons, of all sizes and shapes, covering the ground.

'Have you seen my pigeon?' she cried frantically to all the people on the benches.

Of course, they thought she was crazy. All except for a shabby, middle-aged Arab man, who piped up, 'Yes!'

'Where?'

'Come, I'll show you.' He led her into the woods and, just when she was getting a bit uneasy, he turned to her, started unzipping his trousers and said proudly, 'Voilà! I am going to show you *my* pigeon!'

Lavinia fled in horror. But the fright had cleared her mind. When she got back to the spot she'd left Daffodil at, she ran at the flock of pigeons and scattered them. Daffodil, cooing gently to himself, was the only one that stayed on the ground. He was swept up in her arms and taken back home, making little, satisfied noises to himself about his happy outing in the park.

The apartment had a long hallway. Lav would patiently hold Daffodil on her wrist and lower him to the ground in a swooping motion, with the other animals looking on in encouragement, but she didn't have a great deal of success. Daffodil loved being a baby too much to learn to fly. Eventually, he was locked out in the balcony one day by a friend when Lavinia and he went out for dinner. He must have taken flight, or, even more tragically, fallen to his death, because he was gone when Lav returned.

Decades on, she has just rescued another baby pigeon called Myrtille, two days old, who, she assures me by e-mail, is safely sleeping on her son's T-shirt, which she has wrapped around a hot water bottle. Some things never change.

Ducon was entirely a different kettle of fish. He was the funniest and cleverest animal I've ever met, even if I were to include Joshua. Lavinia had originally given him as a present to a boyfriend, Dominique, but he turned out not to be stern enough to meet that particular challenge. Taken to live at his country house, Ducon would spend all night raiding the neighbours' vegetable gardens and would then lope up the stairs to jump into Dominique's bed. After a long sleep, he would come down to the kitchen and bang his empty bowl on the floor for service. There was a huge dog of mixed parentage in the house called Max. Ducon used him as a means of transportation and rode everywhere on his back. Finally, Dominique admitted defeat because Max was on the point of having a nervous breakdown (Ducon even insisted on going fishing with the two of them) and none of his neighbours were on speaking terms with him. So, Ducon returned to Paris and the high life.

I practically lived at Lavinia's house and whenever one or both of us came home, Ducon would leap up and nip us anywhere he could reach. He had immense dark blue eyes and a beautiful ivory and sienna coat. He also had an immense appetite and would eat the most esoteric things: *gnocchi*, potato purée, chocolate chip cookies—anything that was within his reach. Nothing was safe from his eager teeth. When we ate off trays in front of the TV, he would leap from lap to lap, helping himself with abandon. He chased Bunny so often and so long that the poor cat took to perching on the radiator permanently.

Ducon loved showing off, and we loved watching him. He even had a personal litter tray which he learned to use very quickly; he was always nattily groomed. He would jump on to our laps, waggle his ears and thump his back legs as a command to be stroked, at which his blue eyes would glaze over and his body vibrate with pleasure. If we stopped, his back legs would go *thump!* once again.

When he was about three-years-old, Ducon, sad to say, fell sick. I had had many rabbits as a child and was not reassured by the way he was holding his head. Although his appetite remained undiminished, I told Lavinia that I feared it was of no use and assured her that we would put him to rest in the gardens of *Père Lachaise*, even if we had to sneak in at nightfall, so that she could see his grave from her balcony.

But Ducon did not improve. However, true to form, he was hamming it up for all he was worth. By now, Lavinia had lined his bed with the choicest of her sweaters ('So that he can smell me and be reassured') and he lay there, stretched out as languidly as Marguerite Gautier in the last act of *The Lady of the Camellias,* his huge eyes soulful, especially at the sight of the bowl of freshly-made dinner that Lav was bringing to his bedside. There was Mozart on the record player, and only candles lit the room, since Lav thought that electric light was too harsh for Ducon's weakened eyes.

I was away for the Easter weekend at Quillan, and when the train drew in to the Gare d'Austerlitz, Lav was waiting for me on the platform. If not actually dressed in black, she certainly felt like it. Our comedian was no more.

A year later, before I left for India and Lavinia for Italy for the holidays, we were having our traditional pre-Christmas dinner at our friend Danesh's house. The custom was that we would each bring something ready-cooked as the primary objective was to enjoy ourselves and not waste time in the kitchen. After several of Danesh's famous Old Fashioneds, we were ready to eat. I proudly bore in a dish and announced, '*lapin farci aux pruneaux!*', a roast saddle of rabbit stuffed with prunes.

Lavinia jumped up as if she had been shot, burst into tears and sobbed, 'How could you, Tanyusche? How could you!'

Too late, I remembered the dearly departed. Too late, I rushed back into the kitchen and tipped our main course into the dustbin. It took a long time for her to forgive me this act of callousness, and I never again ate rabbit as a belated tribute to Ducon.

Leo, Princess Smoke, and Being in the Dark

BLISS

For Leo

Curled up, an apricot muff on the tea tray,
he unrolls himself to stretch voluptuously,
his face opening in a yawn.

The salmon pink tongue unfurls,
licking the last bit of honey from his dreams
off his whiskers.

Tea-time is past, but he stays there,
warming his flanks on the teapot.
The furry smell of fish drifts past
and his nose twitches:

right; dinner will be on time.
It is good to live in the body,
with the mind free to butterfly;

it is good to feel the sun soak into supine flesh like a drug,
so the bones dissolve in a jacuzzi of purring pleasure.

A full belly

an empty mind

and slaves in the kitchen.

A cat would be crazy to ask for more.

MOST PEOPLE IN THE VILLAGES OF GOA KEPT ANIMALS, BUT EXCEPT for 'foreigners'—a term which, for the native villagers, covered new residents from other parts of Goa, other parts of India, as well as from other parts of the world—their dogs and cats were part of their households, but were not allowed to sleep inside their houses, fed on leftovers and received no medical care. One has to say that, if most of these villagers were poor, it was almost entirely their own fault. Goa is one of the most fertile states in India, but it also possesses the laziest inhabitants. Although almost anything grew in the iron-enriched soil, the Goan villagers were loath to plant it, preferring to grow a single harvest of rice a year and to fish in the rivers.

They had a few coconut trees and a patch of red chillies per household, which gave them their spices; as well as a few cashew trees that produced the fiery local alcohol called feni. They kept a pig to kill for the festive season and that seemed to be the extent of their exertions. They probably were very smart, because they exerted themselves to the minimum, had long siestas and took full advantage of the taverns on every street corner. Going to church, attending weddings and funerals was all the free entertainment available for them, not to mention the fervent interest they took in what their neighbour was or wasn't doing.

However, anyone who didn't have a paddy field or didn't want to keep a pig had to shop at the local markets, which were very expensive, as nearly everything they sold was grown or produced outside of Goa; this meant that the cost of living had escalated at an alarming rate. The auto and taxi drivers wouldn't have dreamed of running their vehicles on a meter—they simply charged a passenger as much money as they thought they could get away with.

When cats belonging to the poorer inhabitants of the village had a litter, they often threw the kittens over the garden walls of larger and more prosperous houses, thus giving them a chance of being fed, if not looked after. One monsoon day, we heard pitiful little cries from the guava tree in our backyard. On investigation, we saw two tiny kittens, one marmalade and one charcoal, clinging to each other in the crook of a branch. While Antonio ran to fetch a ladder, there was a violent clap of thunder and a drenching fall of rain, which dislodged the babies. They fled around the house and ran to the protection of the veranda, where we picked them up and took them inside to dry them off and feed them.

As they were so tiny, Antonio decided to keep them in the garage, which he used as his studio, to protect them from the boys. He was a full-time parent. Besides feeding them and cleaning out the garage at regular intervals, he rigged up a series of rope toys for them along the windows, and before long they were swinging along in the air like a pair of crazy little trapeze artists.

When they were three weeks old, we judged it was time to let them out—not to mention that the garage smelt powerful by now—and put rolled-up newspapers all around the house, to whack the boys with if they tried to attack the kits.

Joshua had made it clear early on that he wasn't interested in anything on four legs, apart from Thomas, and true to form, ignored them completely; but Thomas was a different matter. Peaceable as he was, cats were nonetheless his hereditary enemies and his blood began to boil every time he saw a kitten—gaily bouncing along the passageway or leaping like a bandit into the room he was in. Many were the whacks he received, but when the kits realized that we were protecting *them* from this fearsome animal, their behaviour rapidly became only what one could call insolent. I had named the marmalade tabby Leo (he was the dead spitting image of my long-lost Romeo) and the little charcoal and black-brindled one was Princess Smoke.

Right from the start it was obvious that Leo was not a bright boy. Not to put too fine a point on it, he was positively simple and a coward to boot. Even a grasshopper could frighten him into a fit. Not such a wuss—Princess was super-bright, but also a terrible tease. She took to walking slowly past Thomas, who would be lying on the floor, his forehead wrinkled and his eyes piteous with the effort of controlling himself. As she came face-to-face with him, like lightning she would swipe with her paw and then stroll away, leaving his nose dewed with blood. Leo would always pad after her at a safe distance and try to imitate her, though his attempts were half-hearted and rarely made contact.

Gradually, after his poor nose began to look like a crossword puzzle, the worm turned and Thomas eventually retaliated, but by this time the kits were fearfully agile and would easily leap out of his way to a safe table-top or shelf. They put him through the mill, but in time, they found other pursuits in the large garden and became absorbed into the life of the house. Leo's life revolved around his meals, which were served often and copiously by his servant Antonio, and he soon decided that he only liked fish.

To this day, I find my gorge rising when I smell fish being cooked, because Leo was capricious and Antonio tireless in his search for the perfect variety to satisfy him. Endless species were cooked—with or without gravy, fried or steamed, spiced or bland, with or without vegetables. In fact, what would have done him the best would simply have been fish guts with boiled rice, which all the local cats thrived on. Naturally, Leo developed into a prima donna, either spurning dish after dish that Antonio prepared only for him, or tasting just a bite of his meal, or gobbling it all up, when the fancy took him. Antonio indulged every mood: only anxious to find the magic combination.

One morning he set out for the fish market at 6 a.m. because Leo had refused the calamari he had cooked for his breakfast. He claimed that as they had been frozen before he had cooked them, Leo was upset because he would only touch fresh fish. I let him go, only pleading with him to get something for our own lunch, as the fridge—except for the calamari—was empty.

The Princess preferred her meat cold-blooded. There was a fine selection of snakes and reptiles of every sort in our huge garden and she became an expert at stalking and catching them. This diminutive killer, with her dish face and huge emerald eyes, was often to be seen swinging a grass snake around her head like a lariat and then bashing it against the garden gate to give it the *coup de grace* before settling down at leisure to delicately devour it. Leo was twice her size, if we compared their weights and heights, and no wonder.

One day we noticed that Joshua had begun banging into things. He had hit the right side of his head on a cement post when he was little, but at the time this had seemed to have had no side effects. However, we now noticed anxiously that his right eye had begun clouding over. The progression of the cataract was horribly rapid, as was our growing fear that he might be going blind. Very soon, both his eyes were affected. Visits to the vet and countless different brands of eye drops seemed to make little difference.

I can hardly bear to think about that time in Josh's life. As his sight failed, he would sit on the sofa, rubbing his eyes in bewilderment and combing his ears over them, always a sign of emotion. The sense of helplessness we felt only made the whole situation worse.

At that time, there was no veterinary equipment in Goa to test dog's eyes. I finally prevailed on my ophthalmologist to examine Josh. Having sworn me to secrecy, he came over one evening. On his instructions, we had given Josh special eye drops to dilate the retina and kept him in a dark room. His verdict was that the disease was congenital.

Researching this diagnosis, we found that most of the kennels in India (despite whatever they put on the dog's pedigree certificate) practised inbreeding in their kennels as a matter of course, because it was cheaper than paying for the stud fees. This led to a weakening of the strains in the bloodline, and in time, to all sorts of diseases; most common among cocker spaniels were blindness, enlarged hearts and unsightly warts. We also discovered that most of the cataract operations done in India at veterinary hospitals and colleges were experimental and carried out on goats.

There was, apparently, one vet in Chennai who did cataract operations on dogs, but the procedure called for a two-week convalescent period, during which the dog shouldn't be allowed to touch its eyes even once. Even imprisoned in an Elizabethan collar, Joshua was so headstrong that there was no way that he could be prevented from doing whatever he wanted, unless we bound him hand and foot for fifteen days. An added complication was that, at six years of age, he already had an enlarged heart, which would make giving him complete anaesthesia for the operation very risky. Laser surgery at that point was not used for animals in India.

I simply couldn't afford the risk of him not surviving the operation, and the vet in Chennai, after she was sent digital photos of Josh's eyeballs, agreed that it was better not to intervene. A visiting friend from New York, who happened to be an excellent vet, told us that unless the retinas of his eyes were viable, the removal of the cataracts would have no effect on Joshua's sight. Alas, the machine that verified this was only available for humans in India, and not for dogs. We tried everything, even after the vets had given up on Josh.

There is a superstition in Goa about the evil-eye, and many people are believed to have it. Some people are said to possess it inadvertently, without bearing any ill will towards the victim.

My grandmother had told me amazing stories about this and how, after the power of the evil eye had been 'removed' by someone qualified enough to do it, the victim had instantly recovered. However, when a person who *does* possess the evil eye lays that villainous eye on someone, he or she—it generally turns out to be a woman, however—is jealous of, the person often falls ill or has something bad happen to them. A friend suggested that we would lose nothing by trying to remove the evil eye from Josh, if indeed, he had been subjected to it.

There are many methods to remove the curse. We paid for the services of one of the village women, reputed as an expert in these matters. She sat Joshua on the green picnic table in our garden and lit a small fire beside it. Chanting in Konkani, the local language, she then waved handfuls of red chillies in a circular motion in front of his face, before moving her hands all over his body, as if cleansing it of the infection. The chillies were then flung into the fire. More chanting, accompanied by more ritual cleansing motions with herbal leaves and lemons followed, with the woman paying special attention to the eyes. Josh was thrilled at all the attention, but nothing changed.

Then my hairdresser Roma, who was also my medical advisor, told me of a spring in a nearby village; it apparently had miraculous healing properties. Her mother-in-law, she said, had recovered her sight after bathing her eyes in the spring water for a month. Antonio immediately set off with industrial-sized plastic bottles to avail of this magic, and we commenced to lave Josh's eyes with the water—which did, indeed, taste very good—every time we could catch hold of him. It was to no avail, although we persisted for at least three months.

There are no words adequate enough to describe Joshua's bravery at having so abruptly lost sight of the world. It really brought home to us the complete truth of how he lived a day-to-day existence, as children do. Something that seems impossible on Monday is accepted as matter of course on a Tuesday, and both animals and children adjust, as if this were the way things always have been.

With amazing rapidity, as he moved towards being in the dark forever, Josh learned to navigate his way around the house and the garden of the villa we lived in. His vet assured us, that in these circumstances, his senses of smell, sound and balance would grow sharper each day to compensate for his lack of sight. This turned out to be the case, but even after eight years, we still put three different varieties of eyedrops in his eyes every day, if only to comfort ourselves that we haven't given up the hope of a miracle.

We discovered that he could follow us by the sound of our voices, especially if we clapped our hands. He soon learned the layout of every room in the house, found his water bowl without any difficulty, not to mention that he could jump on and off the sofas or beds, as in the good old days. His sense of hearing, smell and balance grew in proportion to his loss of sight. He knew immediately if one of us had left the house and would run to the front gate to welcome us back, minutes before we actually arrived. Naturally, with all the constant fussing, he became, if possible, even more demanding. What he had wanted immediately before he now wanted, as the advertising men say, yesterday. We felt, of course, that we could deny him nothing.

Antonio, always reluctant to leave home, now refused to leave Joshua alone if we had to go out in the evenings. This, for him, was a blessing in disguise, because it absolved him from attending scores of tedious gatherings, especially the mob entertainments that Goa is famous for—parties to celebrate birthdays, wedding anniversaries, christenings or first Holy Communions. I generally had to go to these events and suffer alone, not to mention the invention of fictitious excuses as to why Antonio hadn't come along. If I were to be believed, he was permanently ailing (his well-known allergy to the heat was already well established) or perpetually out of town for work.

Soon Joshua was running around confidently enough that it was possible to forget, for long periods of time, that he actually could see nothing. In fact, I often found myself saying to him, 'Can't you see what you're doing?' Sight or no sight, he knew exactly what he was doing if it was something he shouldn't be doing, but it took a long while for either Antonio or myself to harden our hearts enough to scold him.

Three Ice-Cubes and an Ice-Bucket

A ONE ACT PLAY, BY THE COMPANY AT THE VILLA, PERFORMED PRIVATELY on 16 January 2005. No other performances followed, by virtue of the plot.

Cast:
Antonio (playing himself)
Arunesh (devoted friend and honoured guest)
Tanya (unusually mute for most of the duration)
Supporting cast:
Joshua (who insisted on standard union wages, as he had a speaking part)
Thomas and the kittens Leo and Princess Smoke (mute)

ACT 1, SCENE 1

A veranda at the villa.

It is 6 p.m., and the three main characters have stumbled onstage after a hard day at the beach with the boys, followed by a late siesta.

(One must explain that, tonight, we have been invited to a dinner being held at least an hours' drive away, to celebrate the first Holy Communion of the son of Joe and Dulcie, members of the extended family)

Tanya: We have to leave in half an hour to be there in time for dinner, given that we're skipping the mass at church.

(Silence from the other two, who are slumped on their chairs, both blearily drinking tea)

Tanya: I said that...

Antonio: I heard you, I *heard* you. Oh God, how many more of these bourgeois rituals, these fascist gatherings, do we have to go to?

Tanya (*soothingly*): I know, I *know*. You also know that I go with you to *your*…

Antonio: Shut up, shut up!

Arunesh (*very softly*): I really don't want to go.

Antonio: Fifteen mins? Can we go for just fifteen minutes?

Tanya: No.

Antonio: I suppose we can't take the boys?

Tanya: No, definitely not. God … that drive ...

(Silence and dusk descend on the village)

ACT 1, SCENE 2

Nobody has moved from the veranda. It is now 6.30 p.m.

Tanya: Eva's birthday last year, I said you were in Mumbai, so I went alone. Angelina and John's wedding anniversary, I pretended I was exhausted. Reggie's fiftieth, *you* had a dreadful attack of flu. Jeanie's birthday ... for God's sake, how can we do it *again*?

Arunesh (*quite loudly*): I *really* don't want to go.

Tanya (*excitedly*): So we won't go! Why *should* we? We *shan't* go! But we'll have to invent a real crackerjack of a story this time and Aru, they'll all believe *you*. So, let's see ... it has to be unexpected, violent and above all, completely convincing ... See, I've already been stung by a wasp three times this year and...

(Everybody is galvanised into fresh life. A plot is hastily concocted, rehearsed and the stage is set.)

ACT 1, SCENE 3

The sitting room, with a view of the hallway.

Antonio: We have to gag you, Tanya, otherwise you'll never keep quiet.

Tanya (*outraged*): Of course I can!

(Aru swiftly removes his four foot scarf and gags Tanya with it; Antonio pushes her into a chair in the hallway and Aru, for good measure, ties her hands to the arms of the chair with the ends of the scarf.

Aru, as rehearsed, hovers in the sitting room with an ice-bucket filled with rocks, while Antonio goes to the phone and starts dialling. Joshua, discovering that his mistress is trussed up, starts to bark).

Antonio: (*as he had hoped, it is Dulcie who answers the phone*) Dulcie, Dulcie, our wonderful Tanya got stung by a wasp in the garden while she was hanging out the clothes ...

Dulcie: Right *now*?

(Aru is thudding up and down the room)

Antonio: No, no, two hours ago, and we were just about to leave now, when she started swelling up with hives and, shut up, Joshua!

Aru (*shouting*): She's fainted! Oh, she's fainted!

Dulcie: Oh my God!

Antonio: Aru, get some ice … some ice, please get some ice...

(Joshua by now has his paws on his bound mistress' lap, and is barking hysterically, convinced it is all a wonderful game—as, indeed, it is.)

Aru *(rattling bucket)*: I'll get it to her! I'll get it!

(Tanya starts banging her chair, rhythmically against the wooden door of the sitting room.)

Dulcie *(by now thoroughly unnerved)*: What's that noise?

Antonio: The doctor, the doctor ... should I ... who's seeing to Tanya?

Aru *(practically bawling into the receiver)*: Three ice cubes! There are only three ice-cubes left!

(Joshua abandons Tanya and attacks Aru in a flying tackle. There is a dreadful crash as both, ice bucket and rocks, hit the coffee table)

Dulcie: What's going on? What's going on?

Antonio: Tanya, Tanya, hold on, I'm coming!

Aru *(hoarsely, from the floor)*: Three cubes, only three cubes!

(Tanya finally manages to rip the scarf off and produces a piercing scream, at which Antonio slams the receiver down. Aru gets painfully to his feet and carefully takes it off the hook)

Tanya: Biryani for dinner and drinks coming up for everyone!

(Antonio puts Diana Ross on the stereo. Aru lights a cigarette. All the four-leggeds get a hefty chunk of walnut and coffee cake each, and a wonderful evening is had by all, except Joshua, who wants to do it all over again)

A Home of Our Own

I WOULD HAVE BEEN PERFECTLY HAPPY RENTING A PLACE FOR THE rest of my life, but Antonio wanted a house of our own. At nearly sixty-five, I figured he was entitled, so I agreed, only insisting that we live by a river. After what was really a very short search, we found a piece of land on a hillside, overlooking a river in a village close-by, and proceeded to build the house of Antonio's dreams.

He took Joshua on-site whenever possible, so that he could get to know the place; and soon enough, he was racing up the hillside as if he had always known the terrain by heart.

Antonio terraced the entire hillside behind the new house to make it easier for Joshua to navigate and very soon, as he was running down the hill and reached a spot where he sensed—or knew—a slightly steep drop, he would stop short in time and bark until we came to lift him down.

It was a ravishing village we had chosen, approached by a little bridge, with a river on either side of the village.

There were gently rolling forested hills, plateaux covered with wildflowers and innumerable winding roads for walks. When the house was finally finished in 2007 and we moved in, Joshua had all the space he could possibly want. It was a house with lungs—every window opened onto green; it was sweetly shadowed by trees and the garden was loud with birdsong from 3 a.m. to dusk.

Now that we had ample space, the stream of house guests—mostly our friends from abroad—re-commenced, but this time around they were practically back-to-back visits and Josh's life became a continuous party. Best of all, it was a continuous party in his own house, where he could go to bed whenever he felt like it and wake up again whenever he was refreshed enough to resume partying. The only problem was that, as we left our bedroom door open for him to go in and out as he pleased, Joshua simply refused to understand why our guests weren't as accommodating as we were.

They grew accustomed to being awakened in the morning whenever Josh chose to start a series of anguished moans outside their doors, followed by—if that didn't work— volleys of demanding barks for them to open the door and play with him. The bed in the guest room was high too, so even if the sleepy guest opened the door to let him in and then stumbled back into bed, he would bark, 'My pedigree is long, but my legs are short! Lift me up!'

Many of our guests were not animal lovers, but the other attractions of our hospitality, not to mention those of Goa, outweighed their hosts' intense involvement with their darlings. A novice mistress in a convent said of the new arrivals, 'They come and they go, but mostly they go.' In our case, not only did they come, and *keep* coming, but they stayed!

The neighbourhood was safe enough that we even left the front door open at night, for Josh to go into the garden to play by moonlight. Thomas, almost twelve-years-old by now, spent his nights snugly on a sofa he had appropriated for his own use—forcing us to watch TV in the same room on uncomfortable chairs, but never mind that—and in the daytime, he spent more and more hours baking in the sun. The heat, however, was something we never were reconciled to: every successive summer seemed to push the thermometer several notches higher.

I started clipping Josh practically to the skin. At first, he looked like a shorn lamb, but we soon were used to it—but not him. Ever since his one, single mating, he had gotten very bolshy about the monthly haircut and put up a terrific fight every single time. I had to hold him on my lap while someone else clipped him, or vice versa. The whole procedure, which took over two hours, had to be accompanied by my entire repertoire of songs and punctuated at intervals by pieces of cake, given to him as a reward.

It was a tedious process, but I have to admit I enjoyed the songs, which had all been taught to me by my mother. Singing to Josh as his curls of hair fell to the ground, I also regularly rediscovered the flavour of my own childhood. We would always start with the much-loved story of the miller:

There was a jolly miller once
Lived on the river Dee.
He worked and sang from morn to night
No lark more blithe than he.

And this the burden of his song
Forever used to be:
'I care for nobody, no, not I!
And nobody cares for me!'

Then followed, among many others, '*Oh, Jemima, look at your Uncle Jim*', '*Oh, Susanna*', '*The Camptown Races*', '*O my darling Clementine*', '*Mama, may I go out dancing?*' '*Ma, he's making eyes at me*', but we always had to finish (while the last ear was being shorn) with Joshua's very 'own' song, which I had made up for him, to be sung to the tune of David Bowie's '*Here's to the girl who gets a kiss/ and runs to get another*':

Joshie is a Pasha boy
Pasha boy a Joshie (× 2)
Pasha has a castle of gold: (× 3)
It all belongs to Mommie.

Pasha has a thousand wives
Thousand wives has Joshie (×2)
Mommie's chosen every one (×3)
A mob of screaming lovelies.

Pasha's wives are in a rage
In a rage with Joshie (× 2)
What's the use of having a boy?
What's the use of having a king?
What's the use of having a man—
If he only loves his Mommie?

Finally, pouring with sweat, I would bathe, dry, powder and brush him, take a bath myself and then collapse with a strong drink.

As each sweltering April was followed by a scorching May month, I took to keeping a plant sprayer in the fridge and spraying Josh and Tom with iced water every couple of hours.

Only the breaking of the monsoon in mid-June every year brought a temporary reprieve from the heat, though it had its own shortcoming of four months of perpetual rain.

By 2009, such was the global climate change that, apart from the monsoon, we enjoyed only two months of relatively cooler weather, from mid-December to mid-February.

Josh was now ten years old and showed absolutely no diminution in the amount of energy he displayed. In fact, he was as compact as a little bull, and seemed indefatigable in his thirst for entertainment. Whenever I protested at Antonio's catering to Joshua's every whim—walks starting at 6 a.m. and continuing whenever he felt the urge for them; drives after tea to distract him; picking him up whenever he was restless and endlessly talking his special brand of nonsense to him to soothe him—Antonio would say, 'Do you remember Al Pacino in *The Scent of a Woman*? How he used to shout, "I'm in the dark here, I'm in the dark!" Well, so is Joshua—close your eyes and imagine how that would feel if it was going to be for forever! If I could give him my own eyes, I would.' Faced with such a statement, that too from an artist whose eyes are his most precious possession, what could I possibly say?

Every day at twilight, especially when he felt happy—which was nearly all the time—Josh would sit on the veranda and bark his news to the neighbourhood. I had read, in

101 Dalmatians, about this very method that the dogs used to communicate with each other and now I firmly believed in it.

I often think of Joshua in his favourite spot on the veranda in that house which we were soon to leave, four years later, soaking up the dying of the day ... all around him the falling dew; the water buffaloes by the river were feeling for grass with their tongues now that they could no longer see; the pigs in the backyards of the houses were sleeping as quietly as stones.

He would have heard the whirr of the owls' wings as they started off for a night's hunt and all the minute squeaks of the night insects and small animals filling the air. The rustling of the coconut palms in the warm darkness must have soothed him, as well as the familiar sounds from his house, right behind him—music, laughter and the clink of glasses and plates.

The peace of the night must have entered deep into his being, for he would stretch out on his back on the floor, groan in satisfaction, prop a back leg against the wall for added comfort and fall asleep himself, paws crossed on his chest—like a knight taking his well-earned rest, at one with his world.

Mothers and Sons

EVERY WEEK, I WOULD SET OFF TO SPEND A DAY AND NIGHT WITH my mother, now a widow, living in the capital city of Panjim, about an hour away from home.

Antonio would work up to this weekly visit, saying, several days in advance, and also at regular intervals, 'Your mother's leaving us, Joshua, she's leaving us,' at which point Joshua, of course, would start howling in heart-rending fashion.

Antonio would interrupt the cosy evening I would be having with my mother by calling us up and saying that Josh refused to leave the veranda and come to bed: he was waiting for me to come home.

'Here, speak to your mother, Joshua,' he would say, 'She's far away and not coming back until tomorrow'; at which point of course, Josh would obediently moan into the receiver at his end.

There was always some strange crisis that conveniently occurred while I was away each week: power cuts that crashed the computer, a flash flood, an important call from abroad that was cut off, an unexpected visitor who only had an hour to spare and who had urgent business with me. It was strange that, when I was home, none of these things happened. But life is a mysterious matter and is seldom completely understood by us.

Joshua needed both of us with him at all times to be perfectly content, which meant, of course, that Antonio and I had never been away together ever since he had entered our lives. This was not actually a deprivation for me. Antonio had spent nearly all his life travelling—from university in Canada, to four years on the island of Crete, to remote villages in South America, from Morocco to Spain, from Lisbon to Hong Kong. He revved up for each trip he took like a soldier going into unknown enemy territory. Anything might happen to him, and it frequently did.

I was quite happy to make short trips to Bangalore to see Sarojini and to stay home the rest of the time. Sarojini, retired from a long and arduous world-wide career at UNICEF and the UN, now spent her time cultivating her garden, in all senses of the word. She had also acquired a beautiful dachshund, called Dash, whom she adored. It is a measure of her love for me—and true love, as we all know, always contains a fair amount of blindness—that she called me when Dash was about four months old and asked for advice on how to train him. 'He simply won't listen to me,' she would say, in her velvety voice, 'What do you think I should do?' This advice was asked of me; I who had the worst behaved dog in India!

Dash did not take kindly to my relationship with Saro. A sleek and sprightly young man by now, he was not used to his beautiful Roman nose being put out of joint, or being ignored while Saro and I talked and talked and talked—and to each other and not to him. At every visit, I would be smartly bitten by him, and sometimes quite badly so.

Then I had a revelation. After all, he was male. My grandmother, who had dealt successfully with a strong-minded husband and seven children often told me that, when handling a man, flattery worked every single time. 'When I want to do something,' she would say, in her musical voice, 'I always pretend that it's all his idea in the first place and compliment him on his cleverness. Never argue. When he proposes anything, just say, "How wonderful! I would never have thought of that myself!" He'll be so pleased at the compliment that after that you can go and do whatever you want, and he won't even notice.'

I decided to apply her wisdom right away. The next time I visited Saro in Bangalore, I stayed outside the front gate when I arrived. As expected, Dash rushed out, bared his teeth and flung himself against the gate, growling as ferociously as he could for such a small chap. I just looked at him and said, loudly, 'Dash! What a clever boy you are. And so handsome! You look absolutely gorgeous!' Dash dropped down on all fours, stunned at this flood of compliments. My peaceful dove-like attitude, crossed with a serpentine trickery continued, 'I've never seen such a beautiful and brilliant boy! Look at you!'

Dash unclenched his jaw and started to smile. As I continued my litany, his tail slowly started to wag. I then took out his present of chew sticks from my bag, and said, 'The very first present is for you, Dashu-bashu.' The war was over. He took the chew sticks from my hand and licked it.

Of course, I have to repeat this charade every time I visit, as old habits die hard, but we are now as dear friends as it is possible to be, given that we both want the attention of the same person.

Joshua too, by now, had a well-established set of rituals. The boy was fixated on his routine and couldn't bear any disruption in his daily round of pleasures. He had to go out for his walk as soon as he awoke. The teatime biscuits had to be instantly followed by another walk. After each treat, he headed for the garden to celebrate. As he loved grass, we had planted a small patch of lawn just for him, and he would spend happy moments rolling luxuriously on it, tearing up the soil and then flopping over and falling into a dreamy doze. After lunch, he would jump on Thomas' sofa and wreck it, flinging the cushions around and barking with exhilaration. We had to say, 'I see you, Josh! I see you, clever boy!' before he stopped. Many covers we had to darn; many cushions that had had the stuffing knocked out of them. Whenever he was particularly happy, he would repeat this ritual on a bed, scrabbling at the covers with groans of pleasure. Our guests and ourselves soon got used to darned coverlets and patched quilts.

He seemed to feel it was necessary for us to share all this, as if he felt that, apart from himself, he also had to give us pleasure. But unlike us, Joshua gave thanks not for what he was about to receive but for what he *was* receiving, extracting every drop of enjoyment from it.

Antonio would watch Joshua and say, 'Give me some of your contentment, my boy.' Josh would look up at him and reply, 'Yes, when you've been civilized as long as I have been. In the meantime, scratch my stomach!'

Antonio hated being parted from his menagerie and, even when he had to show his face at one of his own exhibitions outside Goa, cut down on his absences to a minimum—one day to hang the show, one day to *open* the show and, without spending any time pressing the flesh or cultivating art critics and journalists (alas, so necessary in today's commercial art world!), beat a quick retreat back home. This did him no good professionally, quite apart from the fact that—neither of us being technologically gifted—he had no website that showed his work. I at least managed to use the computer, but the extent of my skill was simply to write on it. Luckily, we were now in a place that was a trendy holiday destination and, slowly, collectors of Antonio's work and their friends began to visit his studio at home—to look, to buy and to spread the word. This was really a gift from the fairies that look out for old-fashioned dreamers like us, and we were duly grateful to the powers that be.

What of Leo and the Princess? They had moved house with us, but the Princess abandoned us after just one day and took off into the wilderness. The lure of the unknown must have been too much for her. Also, it was a village rich in snakes, chameleons and giant lizards—a smorgasbörd, in fact, for such a connoisseur. We had no fear of her not being able to look after herself.

Leo, of course, didn't budge.

However, the approach of rivals was laying a long shadow. The farmer next door, a saintly young man with a large family, fed any strays with whatever food he could spare. One of his cats who couldn't resist our kitchen windowsill—which looked out onto his garden—was a little brindled cinnamon-coloured beauty we called Mistinguett, after the French cabaret singer. This was soon shortened to Little Miss, or Missy—which both the singer and my niece Mallika were affectionately called—as she grew more confiding. What was extraordinary about her was that she had a bobtail, like a rabbit. I had never seen anything like it on a cat before.

Missy turned out to be the original tart with the heart of gold. Although she looked like a baby, we'd been told that she'd already had three litters. Her lovers were a fearsome bunch, culled from the underworld of the village: they had missing ears and eyes galore, were of all colours but were generally hefty and mangy. Most of them had practically no foreheads, a sign of low or little intelligence. Blood curdling yowls would split the night as they battled for Missy's favours. I have to assume that she didn't put up much of a fight, because she was soon pregnant again.

By this time, she would come into the kitchen to be fed but kept a wary eye out for Leo, who was seething with jealousy. He took to sitting on top of the oven so that he could watch the windows on either side of the kitchen at once, constantly swivelling his head like a lighthouse beam. Missy would only enter if there was someone in the kitchen to protect her from him while she ate.

She had a new litter of two kittens, both snow-white. One of the band of lovers was a dirty grey that must once have been white—clearly, he was responsible. Of the kittens, one had a long tail, but the other, who had a blue and a brown eye, had a bobtail, just like his mother. We were entranced by this little scrap, named him Little Billy and adopted him.

Leo's purgatory had begun. The two cats were rivals indeed.

Leo preferred the last verse of that song, which ended: '*One is one, and all alone/and evermore shall be so.*'

The Return of the Prodigal

BILLY THE KID

O Billy, Billy, Billy
you wild, crazed boy;
with one blue eye
and one eye brown.

Billy Bilbao with the corkscrew tail,
bathed in colour of milk which is only slightly sooty.

Billy Budd,
born in the hedgerow,
you cheeped to me outside my kitchen window,
strange fledgling, open-mouthed with need.

I had to give you away at five weeks,
to someone on the other side of the village,
because my own cat was jealous.

You escaped
and let your pink nose guide you home.

The thread of my love
pulled you across roads like rivers;
over hills that must have seemed mountains to you;
through acres of high-grass
and battlefields of forests.

You soldiered on—
tiny white mouse,
little bird,
little Billy—
until, three days later,

you leapt into the light of my kitchen
and into my astonished arms
and your thunderous purr in my ear
was every love song I had ever heard
in one triumphant shout.

WHEN HE WAS ONLY FIVE WEEKS OLD, I WAS FORCED BY LEO'S bloody-mindedness to give Little Billy away. Leo, who had no respect for fair play, had already tried to kill him several times and, before he succeeded, I had to take action. One of the ladies in the village had recently lost her cat and had fallen in love with Billy when I introduced them to each other. So, I fed him, boxed him and handed him over to her with a heavy heart.

She told me later that he was so friendly when she got him home that she let him out of his box right away. He sat on her lap, had a second dinner, and then went to sleep in a basket she had prepared. But he was gone in the morning. Search and call for him as she might, there was no sign of Billy at all that day. I was terribly upset, because he was so little and spent a miserable couple of days imagining all the dreadful things that might have happened to that little scrap.

Antonio was out of town for a show, so I had to bear it alone. On the third night of Little Billy's absence, I went into the kitchen for a drink and heard a pitiful meow from the patio outside. I threw the window open and Little Billy leapt into my arms, put his paws around my neck and wailed and wailed out his woeful tale to me. It was a terrible saga.

The house he had been taken to was on the other side of the village, and it was incredible that, at only five weeks old, he had found his way back home across that unfamiliar terrain of roads and rivers and fields. I was never going to let this faithful soul go again.

Fortunately, Billy grew up to be thrice Missy's size and quickly put on almost as much weight as Leo. As most adolescents do, he treated me roughly. He also treated the house increasingly like a free restaurant and had an enormous appetite. Very quickly, he learned to recognize the sound of the microwave and would leap through the kitchen window and land on top of it soundlessly, his voice lowered to a deep purr, like Dean Martin after a couple of whiskeys. A true sensualist, he loved the vibration of the machine and would sniff the air appreciatively as his bowl was being warmed up. I had banned all fish for the new cats—they were perfectly happy with their mince and rice, although Antonio insisted on adding fresh herbs, garlic and other spices to it.

Billy was madly affectionate too, which took the form of painful 'love bites'. When he was fully fed, he would drop down on the floor, link his paws around our ankles and whirl himself around like a Catherine wheel. He was an absolute charmer. And Leo was a very, very unhappy boy. He now had to keep watch for *two* rivals, but Billy was more than a match for him, and Leo was too much of a coward to risk a fight. In his misery, he even took to waiting in doorways for Joshua, putting out a paw to trip him up. I think he brooded over his sins until something in his brain finally snapped.

One day, when Billy was about a year old, Leo could stand it no longer. It was now or never! He waited until I was writing in my library, with Billy deeply asleep on the sofa behind me. He must have crept in through the door, left ajar, and jumped on a helpless enemy. The next thing I knew, there was a ball of ginger and white flying across the room and emitting ear-splitting shrieks.

'Out! Out! Out!' Leo screamed, 'Out of my life, out of my house! Out! Out!'

'Get off me, you sick bully!' gasped Little Billy, 'I'll never give in!'

Leo by now was tearing at Billy and scraps of white fur were floating in the air before I managed to separate them with a hardback copy of *Gone with The Wind*. Naturally, I whacked Leo with the hardback, snatched Billy up and slammed the door behind the culprit. Not content with being jailed for three whole hours, Leo crouched behind doors all afternoon, waiting for his prey to give it the kiss-off.

When Billy—who looked a sight, as I had had to dab mercurochrome all over his wounds in a striking pattern of red dots on white—went past, Leo jumped on him again and tore a chunk of fur off his neck. This time, he got a well-deserved whacking with a rolled-up newspaper and retired, snarling with rage, to his post on top of the oven, brooding over his next move. I wanted to dock him his dinner, but the thought of what Antonio would say—he was away yet again—stopped me. I gave him his fish as usual, though he spurned it with a rude gesture and narrowed his eyes at me menacingly.

That night, the criminal disappeared. Though I thought that this was good riddance and was well pleased, I nevertheless roused the neighbourhood so that, when Antonio came back home mid-morning, the hillside rang with people calling Leo's name with an increasing lack of enthusiasm.

'He'll listen to his Daddy!' cried Antonio, ever gullible, and rushed up the hill shouting for his baby. But Baby had clearly had enough of this ungrateful household who welcomed interlopers.

So, Little Miss and Billy had the undisputed run of the house. Little Miss, in fact, had very little brain, but she was so pretty and such a great cuddler that everyone fell under her spell. She simply had to get close to whoever was near her and would then rub herself against them in paroxysms of pleasure, look up with an air of helpless adoration and butt their hands with her head when they ceased to stroke her.

Antonio now turned the searchlight of his attention onto this passionately loving girl. Apart from myself, who was deep into writing my first book of poetry, she was the only other woman in the house and certainly paid him more attention than I did. Missy got what she deserved, according to Antonio: room service. Every ledge in the house was covered with little bowls of delicacies, most of which Billy thoughtfully finished up, so that Antonio would say, collecting empty bowls, 'See how she loves my cooking!'

Antonio's Sunday breakfasts were a feast, which he happily cooked for anyone who happened to be in the house, including the animals.

'It's a holiday,' he would say, 'they deserve a treat.' But, alas, every day seemed to produce a new reason for feeding four-leggeds at the table. Antonio simply couldn't bear to put a morsel into his mouth without sharing it. Every breakfast would see him seated at the dining table with Josh and Thomas on either side of him, ears prickled, drooling in anticipation, and Missy seated cosily at his right hand. One by one, he would feed all three by hand and then put the fourth forkful in his own mouth. I would regularly read the riot act to him, proved by Josh's increasing girth and try to persuade him that he had to be cruel to be kind. He would visibly restrain himself for a day or two, and then crack up and relapse. He was a hopeless case.

By now, we had had Missy spayed, so the mob of suitors had moved on and our nights were quiet, except for Missy purring loudly into either of our necks, and Joshua's snores mingling with my own. Antonio, who was a tidy sleeper, now shared his bed with an orchestra, but the music seemed to agree with him.

However, the climate of Goa did not. His allergies were worsening month by month. We could think of no way to combat them until new friends entered our lives and changed its course and sent us to a totally unexpected destination.

A Dog Named Lorca

By all accounts, the poet Federico Garcia Lorca was not a happy man. The same never applied to his namesake, who was and is one of the most loving and happy-go-lucky souls I have ever met. Lorca was the apple of the eye of a new friend, Rana, who was known to the wider world as the writer Siddharth Dube. They entered our lives in Goa through an introduction by a mutual friend and our mutual attraction was as instant as a bolt of lightning. We had found a true fellow dog-lover; I had found someone I could read poetry with—indeed, Rana chose all the poems for my new book—and Lorca had found a second home. He was a Portuguese water dog, a mass of black curls with a white shirt front and paws. His hazel eyes—exactly the colour of Rana's—were as round as marbles and had an expression of permanent perplexity, as if asking himself what he was doing on this strange planet when he belonged among the stars.

The first time he bounced up our garden path, Thomas stiffened. Always gentle with small animals, he nevertheless needed to let those his own size or larger know what was what on his own home turf. When Lorca saw the look on his face, he instantly threw himself on his back, exposing the length of his soft tummy, in a gesture of total surrender. Thomas, much appeased, sniffed him over extensively. Lorca didn't move a hair, but he was clearly very relieved when Thomas eventually gave him a shove in the side, as if to say, 'Okay, passed inspection! You can get up now, young fellow!'

Lorca seemed to have no defences and no prejudices. He would greet a cat or a squirrel as cordially as he would anything else. Born and brought up in New York, he had then moved to Geneva with Rana, who was working for the UN at that time and had continued his travels first to Delhi and then to Goa. He was at home everywhere and never deviated from the blissful enjoyment of every moment of his life. He was soon as much at home with us as he was in his own and came to spend many holidays with us while Rana was travelling, doing research for the two books he was writing.

The first time Lorca came to stay with us, Rana dropped him off and left. Not a bit bothered by his disappearance, Lorca bounded into the house with his usual enthusiasm and, knowing Antonio, headed straight for the kitchen, where he was given a second—and forbidden—dinner. When it was time for bed, we just put down a rug in our bedroom and said, 'Go to sleep, Lorca'. He lay down, meek as a big woolly black lamb and closed his eyes. He was the perfect guest.

Had it been Joshua in his place...!

A single moment sums up the sweetness of his temperament. I was sitting on our front steps early one morning, putting on my walking shoes. Lorca was sitting by me, leaning on my shoulder. He suddenly gave me a shove with his own shoulder. I turned, startled, to look into his face. His head was cocked to one side, his hazel eyes shining in their tangle of tight black curls and his huge, ear-to-ear grin, showing all of his rose-pink tongue, said, as plainly as anything, 'We're pals, aren't we?'

If he had one defect, it was his passion for playing with balls, a selection of which went everywhere with him. One got accustomed to being awakened in the morning by the sound of a ball being anticipatorily bounced—right by the bed. Or being in the shower and having Lorca come in and bounce it there, quivering with eagerness, tail waving gently from side to side. He could leap up and catch it in mid-air, always brought it back and handed it to you, and could keep up the game for hours without tiring. Any visitor to the house was instantly handed a ball by this indefatigable athlete, much to the relief of our aching wrists.

Rana's courtly and charming father had been one of the most distinguished tea tasters in India. On his retirement, he decided to look for a spot in the blue mountains of the Nilgiris, in South India, to build a house. Ever a romantic, he pitched on a piece of land more than 6000 ft high, right at the top of a mountain. It is true that this mountain was in the middle of a ravishing, perfectly manicured, privately owned tea estate which was also a natural game reserve.

Of course, apart from the few people actually working on or managing the estate, it was an isolated spot, with acres of tea bushes on the rolling hills, shaded by silver oak and eucalyptus trees and an amazing variety of animal and bird life.

Everyone thought Basant was crazy but he was, in his own way, a visionary. Who would have imagined that, two years on, we would have joined him on his mountain?

Rana started the two-year job of building his father's house for him but, barely nine months after Basant moved into it, he fell gravely ill. Naturally, Rana, leaving Lorca with us in Goa, moved to the Nilgiris to look after his father. It was not long before we began to visit to keep them both company. That was when we discovered the Blue Mountains. It was a world out of time.

Ever since I was a little girl, I had always longed to live on a tea estate. Growing up in Calcutta, we had often visited friends living in Darjeeling. The memories of that gracious, spacious life, of rambling white bungalows with gardens crammed with flowers, of clouds coming up from the valleys to blot out those gardens, of the vistas of rolling hills and the fresh, spicy scent of pine needles, had never been forgotten by me. Indeed, if I hadn't gone to Paris when I was twenty-one, I might well have made a marriage of convenience with a tea planter, just to be able to live that life.

That sense of space, of endless time, the marriage of blue and green, the air as sparkling as the spring water—I rediscovered it all over again, thirty years later. My pleasure in this extraordinary landscape was sharpened by everything that I had left behind: heat, concrete and crowds.

By this time, we had been in Goa for ten years and had been witness to the slow erosion of all that we held dear … the extraordinary natural beauty of that state was being defaced by wholesale illegal mining and the irresponsible building of blocks of apartments and gated communities. Rivers were being polluted, forests destroyed and the entire demography of the state was being deformed by the powerful real estate lobby, who were attracting streams of foreigners and super-rich Indians from the big cities to buy up village houses and land. Also, there was a dangerous drug nexus that was flourishing, especially along the beachfronts.

In the old days, no village house closed its doors or windows during the day. The traveller was always welcomed, and offered whatever the household could afford, even if it was only a glass of well water and a slice of fruit. Boundaries were marked by a few stones. Walls were now rising everywhere in the villages to protect properties; bitter battles were being fought over tiny pieces of land, tearing families apart; real estate prices were soaring to unbelievable levels and easy money was the name of the game. We were foreigners in our own 'native land', and no longer felt at ease in Goa.

The second time I visited Rana, his father was visibly fading away. But, like the Cheshire Cat, his smile was the last thing to go: he kept it until the very end—which was, sadly, to be quite soon. The penultimate morning of my stay, I was standing in the garden, which practically had a 180-degree view of mountains rising into the mist, with waterfalls fluting in silver plumes down their flanks into the wooded valleys below. There were herds of wild bison clumped amidst the tea bushes spreading below, and eagles skated the wind: the extraordinary prospect was rather like the opening scene of *The Sound of Music* crossed with *Heidi*. With my feet deep in the long grass, I was suddenly enveloped by a cloud that swooped up the valley and blotted out everything else.

That was when I had my epiphany. As the cloud drifted away, a new life opened up before me, as rich as the landscape all around. A life 'far from the madding crowd', drenched with greenery and birdsong; where the boys as well as us would be rejuvenated by the sparkling mountain air; where we would be able to paint and write in heavenly peace.

I shouted out to Rana, 'We're moving here!'

He shouted back, 'That's the best present I've ever had in my life!'

When I called Antonio excitedly on the phone to tell him about this, all he said was, 'How quickly can we move?' He was clearly as ready as I was.

That was it. On one of our long walks, Rana had shown me a piece of land further down his own hillside. It was nestled below a rockface and looked down the valley to the river far below. There was a spring gushing from the rock beside an immense and ancient jackfruit tree. It seemed made for us. The next month, Antonio came down himself and bought the land. The formalities—unlike the tortuous processes we had undergone in Goa—were over in minutes. We decided to build a cottage and call it Springtree House. In the meantime, we had to find a place to stay for at least a year while our house was being built.

I had already fallen in love with a little rustic white cottage much lower down on the tea estate, with a winding driveway leading to a small secluded garden on several levels. As in a fairy tale, the cottage had two little chimneys, with dormer windows and a red-tiled roof. It was surrounded by jacaranda trees in full lilac bloom. One almost expected Snow White to step out of the door with a broom in her hand, or to see Peter Rabbit hopping round the hydrangea bushes that had blooms as large as dinner plates. As a sign in front of the gate clearly stated that one of the managers of the estate was living there,

I couldn't explore further, but oh! How I envied that lucky man!

They say that sometimes fairy tales do come true.

Auden wrote:

Once in a while the odd thing happens,
Once in a while the dream comes true,
And the whole pattern of life is altered,
Once in a while the moon turns blue.

The Blue Moon

WHEN RANA MADE ENQUIRIES ABOUT WHETHER THERE WAS ANYTHING available for us to rent on the estate while our new house was being built, my fairy tale cottage happened to be the only house that was free. It seemed like fate. I hardly dared believe it was the same place until I was actually able to enter it myself, but that would have to wait. I eagerly accepted to rent it for a year.

We then started our preparations to move from Goa—which seemed interminable while we were in the middle of them, but which actually only took a couple of months. Most of our good friends were taken aback by the suddenness of our decision but understood our reasons. Most of the members of our families thought we'd finally lost it altogether, but that didn't bother us much.

What was most upsetting was Joshua's bewilderment at such a major upheaval. Ever since we had gotten him, our dwelling spaces had been mysteriously growing larger. Our first move with him had been a simple affair of a single truck, with us doing all the packing. This was clearly impossible now, with the huge accumulation of Antonio's paintings and tools, not to mention my 3000-odd books. Beside these essentials, we seemed to have so many unnecessary belongings—all of it had to be sorted, a lot of it had to be given away and the bulky remainder had to be packed by professionals.

Joshua would wander around his house that was being so rapidly dismantled, banging into the cartons the packers were filling up so rapidly. To him, it must have seemed as if everything was changing shape, which left him completely disoriented and with no benchmarks. Familiar furniture had disappeared, doorways were blocked and there were these huge empty spaces where before there had been none. Finally, I put a mattress on the floor in our bedroom, with all of Josh's favourite teddies on it and delegated someone to stay with him there all day. At night, we joined him on the mattress for the week it took for the packers to finish.

The prospect of a straight eighteen-hour drive with the boys then had to be faced. We had decided to do the whole trip at one stretch to get it over with, only making brief pit stops on the way. In hindsight, I don't know now how we did it, for Joshua was now spoiled beyond belief. Anyone who has been told every morning that he is the most precious thing in the entire world obviously believes it. We only had ourselves to blame. Not only had we created Superdog, we had also created Superspoiled to boot. He was the big smell at the top, and he was the boss. At any check, he would put on his obstinate Canine Defence League expression and stick to his guns.

I had to hold him in my lap the entire trip. Not once did he fall asleep, although I longed to myself. In the beginning, it was exciting. We were embarking on a new life in a practically unknown place, and we felt like pioneers. We left Goa at 4 a.m. and saw dawn come up over the sea as we crossed the border into the state of Karnataka. Antonio was in front with the driver; I in the back with Joshua and Thomas in the spacious boot on a thick mattress.

By dusk, we had passed the city of Mysore and had entered the state of Tamil Nadu. As darkness fell, we drove slowly through a beautifully contoured game reserve, ghostly with stands of feathery bamboos. Soon the road started climbing. We could see little in the darkness apart from a scattered twinkling of yellow lights on the slopes of the hills and the occasional groupings of shops and small houses on the main road as we passed little villages along the way. After thirty-seven hairpin bends as the road went steeply uphill, Joshua started hyperventilating and Thomas started panting heavily in the back. After all, they were at the age of almost thirteen and almost sixteen and had never experienced this sort of altitude.

At this point, I truly wished we were back in our house in Goa, on terra firma, with everyone safely asleep in their beds.

But I suppressed my panic, pulled myself together and managed to soothe the boys and promise them that we were nearing the end of the journey. Finally, after 10 p.m., we entered the welcome gates of the tea garden and were on the last lap of the journey to our new home. The cottage embraced us like a lover.

When we woke up the next morning and opened all the doors, they looked out in every direction onto every shade of green, from apple to emerald to viridian. Lemon and orange trees scented the air. The jacaranda trees were a dream of unearthly violet; the fallen blossoms littered the ground like a Japanese painting.

Complete and utter silence reigned. The only sound was the wind in the trees and the charm of birdsong filling the branches, a weaving of many threads. There was the laughingthrush's whistling; the singing of the red whiskered bulbul; the high, sweet call of the purple sunbird. From the eaves of the house, the wood pigeons cooed their immemorial 'Take two, David', and the sun poured down on us like a benediction. I made up a poem on the spot, which seemed to sum it up:

A white bird
In a green tree.

The house was banked against a steep hillside. In front, the garden sloped down to a little road, on the other side of which descended a valley, covered with tea bushes. In the distance the blue mountains rose, with a scattering of red tiled houses across them, where the tea pickers lived.

The stepped garden was bordered by a huge variety of trees: immense silk cotton soon to be in scarlet flower, cherry, apple, pomegranate, guava, frangipani and fir. The colours were Easter colours: white, gold and lilac. There were banks of egg-yolk and white daisies, dandelions bright as medallions, white lilies, lilac crocuses and full-skirted clumps of hydrangea blossoms.

We placed our battered green picnic table and benches under the spreading branches of an old guava tree in the side garden and sat down to drink our tea.

When the sun hit the far mountain ranges before us, they glowed as blue as pansies.

Thomas, as if he'd always been there, found the warmest patch of sun and lay down in it, closing his eyes in thankfulness.

Joshua had no intention of resting: he gave a huge bark and started on a thorough investigation of his new domain, nose snuffling up all the new smells with vigour, exploring every bush and trampling over the flower beds in his enthusiasm. It was easy to forget that his eyelashes were greying, that he had that nasty 'heart' cough, that he couldn't see.

During all those months of preparation, I had held a dream in my head. Besides our desire to leave Goa for a simpler and more solitary existence, I wanted to give Joshua a new lease of life in a world that he could feel even if he couldn't see: a world of heady mountain air spiced by fir trees, of rivers and stars, of clean water and space, of sun on lush grass and the scent of lilies and roses. I wanted him to grow young again on the mountain, to discover a million new smells: new bushes and flowers, different earth, bison dung, bear droppings, dropped porcupine quills and south Indian cooking.

It seemed to be working, because Joshua had on his Native American Indian Chief face: proudly alert, ready for anything as he started digging rapidly in a loamy bed of cosmos as if to unearth hidden treasure for his people. He then flung himself on his back on the succulent grass and started combing his ears forward over his face, a sure sign of intense emotion. We had brought him to the right place at the right time.

Handing on the Torch

JOSH HAD MANY FACES, AMONG OTHERS THE MOULTING EAGLE (WHEN crossed), the bullfrog (when he'd swallowed a mouthful too big for him), the Versace (when he felt particularly well groomed), the glassy-eyed Edith Sitwell (when he was thinking deep thoughts), the General Patton ('Onward, men!'), the William Wordsworth ('but she is in her grave, and, oh/The difference to me!' look when he wanted sympathy), the Rudolf Valentino as the Sheik ('Come, my blossom!'), the Brad Pitt (simply scrumptious) and the Jack Lemmon ('I'm a crazy boy, I am').

He had even more pet-names, but I won't embarrass him by disclosing all of them, except to say that the last one was 'Boo-Boo' or 'Bongo-Bongo'.

The one thing Joshua hated above all was being laughed at. This was actually the only way to silence him but we very seldom had the heart to use this method because the resultant look of shame on his face—the drooping jowls, the averted head, the hooded eyes—was too much for us.

Age had done little to wither him: his coat was still glossy, his teeth sharp, his muzzle, because it was snow white, showed no grey—only his eyelashes and his ears did that—and he was still as compact as a little bull.

There were two problems we all faced at the cottage. The first was the cold. At nearly 6,000 feet above sea level, we began to practically live in tracksuits. It was particularly comforting at night to have the warm bulk of Joshua sandwiched between Antonio and myself like a hot water bottle.

Alas, the new bed was too high for him to jump off and on, and most of our own furniture was in storage while the cottage was fully furnished. When he had developed his disturbing cough in Goa, it was exacerbated by any sudden movements, such as a high jump, so we had bought him a really expensive faux leather basket, complete with cushions. When we had introduced him to this new resting place on the floor beside our bed, Josh took it very badly. He naturally assumed that we no longer wanted to spend our nights *à trois*, but he was determined to preserve the status quo at all costs. To this end, he continued jumping on and off the bed at night, bursting into fits of coughing each time, which upset us terribly. One night, I waited till he was heavily asleep beside me before cautiously picking him up and putting him in the basket. He stretched out, turned over and soon I heard a gentle snore. Success at last!

Alas, when he awoke shortly after, he found himself, to his horror, actually in the hated basket. He leapt out, gave it a terrific swipe with his paw and started to try to tear it apart, growling with rage. Luckily, it was too stoutly made to be dismantled even by him. He was mortally offended by our duplicity, and of course, was immediately reinstated in our bed, with all the attendant fits of coughing.

However, now that we were in different climes, the red cement floors of the cottage, icy to the touch, did not lend themselves comfortably to be lain on. In time, Josh reconciled himself to the basket (now cosily loaded with rugs and throw covers) as a daytime resting place in the dining room, where the main activity of the house took place.

At night, however, his place was with us. As I said, the new bed, though larger than the old one, was just that little bit too high for him. Until we had to lift him on and off it, we had never really grasped the extent or number of Josh's nocturnal perambulations. Our nights were now punctuated by regular barked requests from Josh to be lifted down or up, and it was torture to leave the heavenly warmth of the duvet to do this, even for a moment.

However, we had no choice, so whoever was less deeply asleep had to be the official lifter or setter. We were rewarded by the huge sigh with which he flung himself back upon us, followed by a sleepy lick, before he fell asleep again, paws crossed above his speckled belly in perfect peace, his breath warm in our ears as his cheeks puffed in and out like a little steam engine.

The cold was invigorating, but it also sharpened both boys' appetites. Until now—with the exception of Antonio's furtive handouts at table—they had had only one big meal a day at noon and Marie biscuits at teatime. But now, Joshua was shouting for another meal barely an hour after he'd devoured his lunch!

We were watched like hawks at table, even by Thomas. In his desperation, Josh even sampled the south Indian vegetarian staples made of rice flour: steamed cakes called idlis and crepes called dosas, eaten with a variety of spiced lentil stews. He eagerly accepted fruit for breakfast, something he hadn't done since he was a puppy. Antonio started calling him 'Jaws'—the kitchen became his stake out and every fresh noise of chopping or cooking, every fresh smell from the stove or oven elicited pleading moans for nourishment. He put on weight at an alarming rate, and we began to call him Buffalo Bill. At all times, no matter how deeply he was asleep, at the first whiff of a dish being placed upon the dining table, there would instantly be a warm, pleading muzzle placed heavily on my knee and palpable waves of yearning rising up from it.

Even Thomas, who, having been brought up on the streets and fed hand-outs from the locals in Bangalore, now, like Oliver, wanted more. Previously—being basically a biryani and jalebi boy—he would look with deep suspicion on anything 'foreign' like cheese or baked dishes. But now, in this mountain air, he was ready for anything that filled this new void. We eventually settled on an additional evening meal for both of them—chicken broth with rice—as a last resort to have at least a few hours' peace.

The evenings were the second problem. The plantation, as I have said, was the natural habitat for a great number of animals. Besides the jackrabbits, monkeys and the peaceful herds of barking and mouse deer, there were also wild bison, elephants, bears and, the most dangerous of all for dogs, panthers. We heard many stories of dogs snatched by panthers, never to be seen again, because they were light and easy prey for this natural predator.

Because of this, as soon as dusk was approaching, every door had to be closed, and the boys only taken out within the garden on a leash.

It took months for Joshua to reconcile himself to this curfew. All his life, he had been so accustomed to running freely in and out of the house wherever he was, from dawn to bed-time, that he simply couldn't understand why he was now locked in right after his post tea-time walk. Antonio, of course, took him on endless little outings during the course of the evening to try to calm him down.

However, after the intense social life he'd enjoyed in Goa, he was bored in the evenings. He would start moaning. The range and variety of the sounds he produced were so astonishing—as well as maddening—that a friend unkindly suggested we rent Josh out to the local film studios to provide additional soundtracks for Tamil porn movies. Thankfully for the state of our ear drums, many old friends from his past life soon started visiting us, and he gradually came to accept this new life as a happy continuation of his adventurous existence.

Certainly, both the boys had a new leap in their step and a brighter gleam in their eye. They were now hillbillies and up for practically everything—except perhaps the pregnant panther that was currently living round the bend of our mountain.

In this strange, unaccustomed and welcome solitude, Josh and I would sit for hours on the warm grass in the sheltered garden, surrounded by trees incandescent with sunlight, looking out over the blue mountains, his paw wrapped around my arm and his head against my shoulder while we talked about our lives or I read my poetry to him. Life couldn't get any better.

I couldn't imagine our life without the boys. To lose them—especially Joshua—would be like stamping down on the very earth and grave of one's own life. But I think of Byron's words:

For the sword outwears its sheath,
And the soul outwears the breast,
And the heart must pause to breathe,
And Love itself have rest.

From this vision of the grave, the mourning candles and the funeral wreathes, we jump to an evening walk with the boys barely three months after we'd moved into the cottage.

Round the same bend of the road where the pregnant panther was said to live danced a little long-haired mongrel girl. She was about six months old, fawn coloured, with the darkest almond-shaped eyes. Of course, as in all stories of the beggar-maid, she was very thin, had a damaged paw, and all her ribs were visible. This didn't have any effect on her high spirits when she saw us because she greeted us each in turn with enthusiasm. When Antonio bent down and let her kiss him, her plumy tail became a blur of colour. She knew quite well that her Prince had come.

The first evening, she ate and slept. The second day, she was bathed and vaccinated; her wounds were tended to, and she ate some more. The third day she was in Joshua's bed in the morning and our own by nightfall. The fourth day she had to be dissuaded (ever so gently, by her Prince, who lifted her down with great reluctance) from sitting with us at table.

Her name is Ninotchka and Joshua has been the soul of gallantry. So far. Youth must have its fling, he seems to say, when he jumps into his bed and finds a little bundle already curled up there. Maybe it's time to start being an old man now and to take it a little easy.

Time to hand on the torch.

Thomas Speaks

I NEVER KNEW MY FATHER, NOR DO I THINK I EVER HAD ANY BROTHERS and sisters. I remember a special smell and a warmth that enfolded me, but it went away very soon, and I was on my own in a hollow beneath a red-flowering tree. I ate what I could from the dustbins. It was lucky that the park had many of them, because there were houses in a circle around it. I wasn't alone for long. A big dog soon joined me with his gang. He had a black stripe in the middle of his face and I heard my Mistress call him 'Badger' a long time later. Badger was kind to me and I grew very quickly, until I was bigger than him. Not all the other dogs were as kind. There were many that came and went; some of them stayed with a new gang only for some days before disappearing. I don't know why: I was never brave and just wanted to be safe. It wasn't easy to be safe on the streets. Although I was a big dog, I never used my size to bully dogs smaller than myself. We are what we are and we didn't make ourselves. As the months and years passed, I grew lonelier and lonelier. No other dog seemed to speak my language.

I felt that there was a cord attached to my heart and that it wanted to find someone it could be tied to. I liked Badger, but he wasn't the one. Also, he was the boss of the gang, and as time went on, there were many fights as newcomers tried to be the leader of the pack.

As I grew older, I followed them less and less at night when they went scavenging in the dustbins or in the rubbish heaps behind the restaurants. Instead, I started going out on my own in the early mornings, when the air is fresh and the dew is still on the grass. I loved to put my face into a soft flowering bush and breathe in the green smell and then take my face out, all washed and clean. People saw me doing this, and some of them called out to me from their houses, where they were sweeping the pathways or watering their plants.

It took me a long time to answer their calls, but the first time I did, a kind lady gave me a tin plate with rice and fish curry in it. It was so good to eat fresh food from a clean plate and to be alone when I did it! Soon, I had at least three or four houses that I could go to in the mornings and be sure of being fed something if I waited until someone came out of the door. But I still slept with the gang.

One day, a very mangy yellow dog joined the gang. He was in bad shape, and he told us that his owners had gone away a year ago and had left him behind, on the street. He wasn't used to fending for himself and soon got ill. However, his troubles had not made him a better dog: he was bitter and angry and thought that everything that had happened to him was undeserved. Life is like that. If you expect much, you get little. If you expect little, you may get something. If—like me—you expect nothing, maybe someday you'll get lucky.

Yellow, in his misery, began to pick on me because I never fought back. Since he had joined the pack, he was eating better and had started to lose his starved look. But his coat was still rough and diseased. I tried not to get too close to him. Although we were living rough, I avoided mud, rain and nasty places and tried to keep myself as clean as I could.

Yellow would shove me aside if I had found a nice hollow to sleep in and take the place that I had already warmed or, when I had found something to eat, he would snatch it from my mouth. One morning, he saw me leaving the pack and followed me at a distance. When he saw a man putting out a plate of food for me, he waited behind a corner of the house until the man went back inside. I had my mouth full of the delicious taste of rice and chicken skin when he fell on me.

Although I hate fighting, I love fair play even more. For the first time, I fought back.

But Yellow was—as his scars showed—a seasoned fighter. Although I was bigger and heavier than him, he sank his teeth into one of my hind legs and tripped me up. I fell on my side, and he went for my face. His teeth ripped up my muzzle like a piece of cloth and suddenly I couldn't see for all the blood. The pain was like nothing I had ever felt before, and my one thought was to get as far away from him as possible.

I cried for a long time in the dark alley I finally found myself in. I was grateful that there was nobody there and when the pain eventually dulled, I fell into a disturbed sleep. I never wanted to go back to that park or to meet Yellow again. I missed Badger and my familiar old haunts, but that part of my life was over. I found another place by myself—in the same neighbourhood, but at a safe distance.

Two days after the fight, I was sleeping in the doorway of a house. Everything was silent; it was still very early. Suddenly, I felt something being slipped around my neck and I was jerked to my feet. A man was holding a rope attached to the noose around my neck. When he saw that I wasn't going to struggle, he dragged me quite gently to the pavement. There was a dirty big black van standing by the kerb. He opened the back door, picked me up, and threw me in. There were at least six other dogs in there, all tied to a metal screen with ropes around their necks. It was the first time I had been in one of those shapes I saw running down the roads. I was very frightened by the vibrations under my feet and running through my body. I was even more frightened about where I was going with all these strange dogs.

When the van stopped, the back door opened and the man took us out, one by one, into a big room with a white floor on which were big tin tables. There was a lady wearing a white coat who came to me. She stroked my head, and when I blinked and licked her hand, said, 'Good boy'. The man lifted me onto the table and then she cleaned my face. 'What a scar!' she said softly to me as she put something cold on it. The pain stopped at once.

Then I felt something sharp pricking my behind and I couldn't feel anything there any longer, not even when I moved my back legs. The lady made me lie down, and then everything went black. When I woke up, I was in a sort of cage with the other dogs. I only discovered later that they had cut off my balls. It was strange to lose something that was part of me, but I saw that none of the other dogs had any left, either.

I hoped to see the lady in the white coat again, but she didn't come back. We stayed there for some days, but we were well fed at least twice a day. I didn't want to be shut in like this, but the other dogs weren't bad chaps, and I heard lots of stories, both good and bad, but mostly bad.

One morning, when it was still very early, the man came again, and put the ropes around our necks and put us back in the black van. I was very frightened and started shivering. But the journey wasn't long and lo!—when we stopped and the man put us out on the road, I saw that it was the same street I had been taken away from.

From then on, I took good care to hide myself most of the day, except for the early mornings and late at night, when I would go looking for food. I didn't understand anything that had happened to me, nor why. In my bewilderment at everything that had happened to me so far, it seemed to me that the whole of life was a riddle: is there an answer to why a tree or bush is there, or a little flower or a cushion of moss? Any reason for the way all the insects and animals move around in the world, or the people coming in and out of their houses and going about their business? Any answer to why some people and animals are unkind while others are not?

What am I doing in all this and will I ever find an answer? Not until I find someone who loves me and I love them—that will be answer enough for me.

And so it happened that one night when I was very hungry, I went down a street where there were many small restaurants that sold food. I liked the meat place best, where good meat, such as I had never tasted, sizzled on long, thin rods over an open fire. At least I could fill my lungs with that good, good smell and try to forget the growling in my stomach.

When I got to the good smell, there were quite a lot of people waiting in front, but I only saw one person, who caught my eyes at once. It was like I was hit in the heart. I felt as if I had always known that person and that the cord in my heart had finally found a place to attach itself to. It was such a relief! Such a feeling of joy washed over me that, with no thought for anything else, I ran forward and grabbed her wrist—very gently but firmly—in my mouth. She looked down, and I looked up, and there was no more to say. I was hers, and she was mine.

So I came home, where I had always belonged and was happy forever after. I had my own sofa; I could sleep as long as I wanted; my Mistress always asked me if I liked my food, and best of all, I was hugged and kissed and praised all the time until I felt warm inside, as if there was an eternal fire inside me.

They tell me all the time how handsome I am, and their friends do, too. Mistress' mother calls me 'a nobleman'; Venita calls me 'a prince among dogs'; Sherree says that this time round, she will settle for no less a partner than someone who is like me; Diviya says 'Saint Thomas isn't good enough … he should be a Cardinal—why not the Pope!' I don't know what all these words mean, but I know they mean good things by the voices in which my friends say them.

I know my Mistress didn't blame me when I couldn't protect her against that pack of dogs when they attacked Joshua. I can't fight for her, but I will never leave her side. I love her with a love that many waters cannot quench. I like that verse, that she reads out of her blue book with the soft cover that she also strokes my cheek with.

Of course, there was my new brother, Joshua, but, compared to most of the other dogs I had lived with, it wasn't hard to love him. First of all, he was a baby, and I have always had a tenderness for young things. He was so full of love and life that there wasn't a mean bone in his body. When he jumped on me and tried to bite me with his sharp little teeth, it was like ants pricking me and I would wrestle him until he stopped. I enjoyed teaching him how to grow up and he thought I knew everything. Nobody had ever thought that about me. It didn't matter that he never took my advice or followed my example. Life had been easy for him always, and he never thought that anything bad could happen to him.

I know that he was there before me and that made him come first. Sometimes, it is hard to be second best, but my Master always gives me the first bite—before Joshua. I know that my Mistress doesn't do the same thing, but women always love smaller things better, so I try not to mind when she talks to Joshua all the time or kisses him twice as much as she kisses me. The Master says, 'Look at Thomas! Kiss him first, because he was the one who chose you!' And sometimes she does, but mostly she forgets. However, she praises me so much to all her friends, and I never hear her praising Joshua—she only tells funny stories about him—so I suppose I come first there.

I was never a chap given to travelling, but I've never made a fuss when we move the way Joshua does. And we've moved so many times, you'd think he would have gotten used to it by now! I don't know why Joshua started banging into me or falling over me when I was asleep. As I grow older, I get annoyed about this. The Master and Mistress scold me when I snap at him sometimes and say I should be kind to him because he can't see. But what does that mean?

Anyway, now that I am old, I feel I can ask for more things. When there is a thunderstorm in this new, mountainous place we have come to live in, I jump into bed with them. Before, I wasn't allowed on any other bed but mine, but now I sleep anywhere I want to and nobody says anything to me. I have to take a lot of pills, but they put them in pieces of cheese or chicken for me and now I love these treats. My Mistress even makes special biscuits for me, and she calls them 'Thomas' biscuits', and nobody else can eat them, not even when there are no other biscuits in the house and Joshua shouts for one. Joshua's life has always been one of such freedom—even if he is clumsy now and bumps into things—he does whatever he feels like all the time. How many of us are as lucky as that?

Now we have a young girl called Ninotchka who has come to live with us. I am tired now, and I don't have the energy to look after her the way I looked after Joshua. But she is smarter than both of us put together. She was born in this cold air, and it must have sharpened her mind because already, after only a few days, she thinks she can have everything that is ours. But that is the way with women, I have found, although I haven't known very many of them. It is best to let them do what they want to do, otherwise they will never let us live in peace. So, I let Ninotchka eat from my bowl, and I let her sleep on my new, big bed, but I refuse to play with her when she comes barking around me.

I said this yesterday, but today she wouldn't leave me alone.

She put her paws around my neck and swung on it; she jumped on my back when I was sleeping in the sun; she nipped me all over like a little bee. I had to push her off, and that was the beginning of the game for her: she wanted to wrestle. After an hour, I was so out of breath that I had to pin her down and we both went to sleep. Now she shares my bed and puts her head on my chest as if she were my child.

I'm an old warrior and I need my rest, but it does feel sweet to have her warm under my chin at night, and in the daytime, to see a young one taking her first steps towards growing up. Joshua just ignores her, so it's up to me to see that she doesn't get into too much trouble. You should see her chasing the bands of cheeky monkeys that are raiding the guava tree! She doesn't seem to know what fear means.

It's too bad that the Master follows her around all the time, as if he's afraid that she's going to vanish. Not she! Having found a home like this, she'll never leave. She'll live to boss all of us around, just you see!

Sometimes, when my Mistress watches Joshua tearing up another quilt, or the master putting teriyaki sauce and seaweed in our food, she puts her arms around my neck and says, 'Thomas, where shall wisdom be found, and where is the place of understanding?'

I don't think I will ever understand everything, but one thing I do know: Joshua is first in their hearts and the Mistress has explained to me that this is the Book of Joshua, so let it be so.

I have my reward already: he can have all the rest.

Casting Off

THOMAS LEFT US NINE MONTHS AFTER WE MOVED TO THE HILLS. He departed as nobly as he had lived for all his sixteen and a half years.

He had been getting feebler over the last three months of his life but was only really bedridden for three days. He simply lay in his bed in the dining room, in no pain, with his eyes following us. We were so glad that we had brought him here to spend his last months in the peace and cool air of the mountains.

Fittingly, he died on a Sunday. We carried him out into the garden at 9 a.m. and laid him in the sun on a rug in front of an early-flowering peach tree. It was a beautiful blue day, with huge white clouds sailing above. Antonio and I sat on either side of him; Joshua, true to himself, was digging holes in the newly-tended garden, and Ninotchka was chasing the monkeys that were swinging overhead in the jacaranda trees.

We spoon-fed him every half hour and talked to him ... his eyes never closed; they were full of light.

At 2.20, his breathing was getting heavier, and I suddenly wanted to read him the poem that ended Tennessee Williams' play, *The Night of the Iguana*. I couldn't find the book but sat down beside him and tried to recite what I remembered:

How calmly does the olive branch
Observe the sky begin to blanch
Without a sigh, without a prayer,
With no betrayal of despair.

O, Courage! could you not as well
Select a second place to dwell:
Not only in that golden tree
But in the frightened heart of me?

Antonio was holding his head as I continued with Yeats' poem:

I will arise and go now, and go to Innisfree,
And a small cabin build there, of clay and wattles made;
Nine bean rows will I have there, a hive for the honey-bee...

As I reached the last word, this angel—the colour of honey—wagged his honey-coloured tail, stretched out all his four legs to their fullest length, and his amber eyes glazed over. His great heart had given out at last.

We wrapped him in his favourite blanket and put him in the car. I made a bouquet with the first peach-coloured rose from the garden in the heart of it, and Antonio drove him to the site of our new house, where he had already dug a grave under the apple tree the day before. Antonio put him down himself and covered him with the kindly earth.

He shall be the guardian of our house; no house could have a gentler or more faithful presiding spirit.

With the loss of Thomas, Joshua, of course, was ever more firmly planted in the centre of our life and continued to illuminate every single moment of it, even when we had to take him out four times a night. After all, that's what soulmates are for!

We *both* had jowls now but his were far more enticing than mine. As I said at the beginning, neither age nor infirmity diminished his zest for life. In this beautiful place, we both seemed to have drunk of the magic potion and were renewed every day, getting younger at heart as we grew older in body.

In every village, in every city, in every country, stories like ours are being enacted—stories that cross borders, stories brought about by chance encounters, stories that change lives. How could I not try to be a better person with someone like Josh believing so unquestioningly in me and making me feel so special? I really can't say that we learned from each other: Josh went his own way, and as that way is inextricably bound to mine, I followed. Through his eyes I discovered how much more there is to the world than I thought there was. Sometimes, blindness opens eyes that see a different world—a newer world; a better world.

Epilogue

JOSHUA AJAX: 12 December 1998–22 April 2013

A star danced the day I was born

LETTING GO OF JOSHUA WAS THE MOST DIFFICULT THING I'VE EVER DONE in my life. Antonio, with his more generous heart, would have felt it equally for any other—what? 'animal' isn't right; 'pet' is insufficient—let's say for any other vital element in our lives.

But not I. He was my alter ego; my one and only.

I'd grown accustomed to his face … the way he made the day begin (even if he were screaming, as he did towards the end), his smiles, his frowns, his ups, his downs…

In the simplicity of our attitude to life we were as one—we ate, we drank, we made merry. Oh, we were happy as the grass was green.

His cheek against mine and the puff of his breath was all I needed to know to feel blessed.

And all that had to go—into the unforgiving void.

To go—to let go … how does this feel when you have to help the person let go?

Only poetry has the answer. That great poet and dog lover, Mary Oliver, said:

To live in this world

you must be able
to do three things:
to love what is mortal;
to hold it

against your bones knowing
your own life depends on it;
and, when the time comes to let it go,
to let it go.

Fortunately, I had a good amount of luck; I had met a local vet who was kind and gentle, with a lot of experience in dealing with terminal illnesses.

On my way back from a Thursday shopping trip, I looked at the big bag of medicines I'd bought for Josh. Always terrified of running out, I replenished the supply every time I went to town. I looked at it and asked myself, 'Why am I doing this to him?'

He was fourteen and a half, he was practically mainlining the stuff, wrapped in anything that could disguise the taste of the pills. A month ago, in the temporary house we were living in (after we had had to leave the cottage), he'd managed to get through the rope barrier Antonio had constructed across the top of the stairway and fallen down the stairs. Since then, we'd had to lift him up to walk, which he now did with the gait of a drunken sailor, since he had lost all sense of orientation. But he wouldn't give up ... there would be no going 'gently into that good night' for Joshua unless we helped him.

Nobody had more zest for life than Joshua. To the end, despite his enlarged heart, his unseeing eyes, his cognitive disorder and the almost hourly medication he had to take while he was awake, his great heart pumped on. Even when he was crying with frustration, it pumped on.

In his last two weeks, in desperation to stop his frustrated screaming (he was never in any pain, or we would have known), his wonderful vet in Mumbai (who had been looking after him over a long distance for two years) put him under heavy tranquillisers which, knowing his resistance, took quite a while to take effect.

He only stopped crying when something delicious (so little of which he was allowed!) was put into his mouth or he was helped to walk under the jacaranda trees in blossom against the spring sky.

I never knew quite how deaf he was. Naturally, he never listened to any commands, but he always heard the sound of Antonio's footsteps (and mine) and he always heard my voice: no one else's.

I came home that Thursday and spoke to Antonio right away, who had to admit that letting go of the boy was our only way forward. Hand in hand, we went to look at him (he was asleep, for once!). We cried and cried. Then I called Josh's vet in Mumbai and the local vet and made arrangements for the following Monday. I have to say that both of them, however much they empathised (and they did, they did!), must have been exasperated by me in the next few days—I kept calling them to make quite sure that Josh would be in no pain at all and that it would be as quick as possible.

So, for our last four days together we threw the rule book away, and Joshua relived his glorious culinary past. The Royal Canine dog food he had come to hate—and had almost stopped eating—was shoved aside and our boy had everything he could possibly want. He could hardly believe his nose when roast veal with peppers, *boeuf bourguignon* with steamed potatoes and green beans, mixed fried rice, bacon and eggs, buttered toast, chicken stew and lemon cake were put under his nose—he gobbled each meal so fast we thought he would choke in his haste to consume it all.

I put away his piles of medication in a box to give to the vet, as well as all the apparatus—antiseptics, organic haldi, neem pills and oils that we had been using for eight months to cure the abscess on his bottom.

And then, on Sunday night, I told him what was going to happen the next morning. I told him everything while he snuffled against my cheek, and afterwards I had the best sleep I'd had for months.

The next morning, after his 10 a.m. 'lunch', I saw him lying on his back on the floor next to his bed, in his attitude of total pleasure, with all four paws in the air. Our maid said, 'Look, ma'am! He hasn't done that for months!'

I had clipped him the week before while he slept and he'd always had a hot sponge bath every day at noon with all the attendant paraphernalia, so he smelt like a rose.

Despite the piggy way he had eaten ever since he was a baby, he'd always been tremendously fastidious. There was no way I would put him through the humiliation of losing control over his body; he would have hated that.

But the vet, who had to drive three hours to reach us by 11 a.m., had met a roadblock and was delayed. That was a horribly painful forty-five minutes. It is one thing to know that you have to let a beloved go and something else to have that fatal time stretched and strung out, through no fault of anyone's.

Antonio carried Josh out for a last walk and then we put him to bed. He was drowsy; his morning medication had finally started to kick in ; they would be his last.

I had lit a candle in our shrine, to St. Anthony and my mother, early in the morning and the flame was still burning. I had no more prayers to say for our boy, except to ask them to look after him, again at this moment of passage. My head was spinning.

After the vet arrived with his young son, acting as his assistant, everything went very swiftly—too swiftly. I couldn't believe that this marked an end, from then onwards. But I was determined not to leave him, not for an instant, nor to upset him in any way. I wrapped him in my own white muslin towel that smelled of me and put my arms around his neck. Antonio held steadfast to his body from behind. And I sang to him, over and over, his favourite lullaby that my mother had sung to me as a child:

Chi baba, chi baba, chi wawa,
Enjalawa kooka la goomba.
Chi baba, chi baba, chi wawa,
My bambino, go to sleep.

All the stars are in the sky, ready to say goodnight.
Can't you see your doll is sleepy, too?
Close those drowsy little eyes; mama will say goodnight,
While she sings a lullaby to you...

I kissed his soft cheek over and over as I sang and wet that beautiful domed head with scalding tears ... but he couldn't feel them any longer.

The vet later said that it was heartbreaking to watch. Our maid had brought a pile of flower petals with her and each of the others sprinkled a few on Josh's side.

I just kept kissing his speckled belly and asking the vet, over and over, if he was really gone.

'I promise you, he has.'

We said our goodbyes and expressed our gratitude to the vet and put Josh in the car. We drove the ten minutes it takes to reach the site of our new house, where Thomas had already been buried in December, two years ago.

Our contractor had already dug a deep grave in a corner, right next to my future herb plot on a slight rise above the ground; we had quilted the floor with flower petals. Two of the workers climbed down, into the grave, and we handed over Josh to them, still wrapped in my white towel.

As they were gently lowering him down in his white cradle, he seemed to have the strangest expression on his face. He looked like a pup again, all glossy and plump—sleeping as soundly as a baby—*à poings fermés* (his fists tightly closed); he looked as if he had secret, a huge and a happy one, deep, so deep in a dream. Antonio covered him with an emerald green towel. Each of the fifteen or so workers showered him with a handful of petals. I left to sit on the veranda close by; I couldn't bear to watch him being covered with earth. When the grave had been levelled, Antonio and I placed a circle of round slate stones from our site on it and filled the circle with tuberoses.

I had copied the burial service from the 1662 Anglican *Book of Common Prayer* and I read out excerpts. I had to stop at many moments, but it didn't matter how long I took, it didn't matter any longer.

'...*For a thousand years in thy sight are but as yesterday: seeing that is past as a watch in the night.*

...*Behold, I shew you a mystery: We shall not all sleep, but we shall all be changed, in a moment, in the twinkling of an eye, at the last trump: for the trumpet shall sound, and the dead shall be raised incorruptible, and we shall be changed.*

...*Then shall be brought to pass the saying that is written, Death is swallowed up in victory.*

O death, where is thy sting? O grave, where is thy victory?'

At the very end, I showed him his book, *The Book of Joshua*, and told him how much he had been loved, especially by people who didn't even know him in the flesh.

I read him a last poem:

You're closer to me than a cheek on a pillow;
You're nearer to me than the beat of my heart;

You're more welcome than beauty in everyday faces;
You're dearer than sunlight,
My little sun.

You're sweeter than honey sucked from the honeycomb;
You're brighter than stars and wilder than storms;
More complete in your loving than the circle of reason;
I breathe out; you breathe in,
My little sun.

We then had to leave him; we returned to our temporary home, and there we stayed until we moved into Josh's new home at last.

There is a rosebush over his grave now, which had been growing wild on our site ... it has large blooms that are parti-coloured: yellow and crimson; and soon he shall have a gravestone.

But these are small offerings in return for everything he gave us, all throughout his lovely life.

He deserves all my grief.

I know I shall make a different life for myself; a life without him; a life with new pleasures, new meeting, new rewards. But, at the centre of the heart, there will always be a space that nothing else can fill.

Between us, there was never that particular difference that the French say there always is between lovers—that there is the one who kisses, and the one who is kissed—we both kissed each other with equal fervour.

There was only one difference between us: I loved only him, he loved the whole world and everything in it.

Grief, however great, is eventually transmuted into something else … months later, in our new home, I saw Joshua again on one of my early morning walks and wrote this poem, which sums up our love, and which had then reminded me that ours was eternal.

Joshua Comes Back

He comes hurtling across the shining surface of the world
sunrise dazzle blind the eyes
that thought him lost six months ago.

But no:
the silver meteor has become a body
the body a barrel
the barrel a beloved bundle of black and white patches
that crashes round the bend.

I see the windmill ears
the mouth roaring open to eat the wind
the heart that I can hear from here
of this runner who breasts the tape to me

and as he hits me like a cannonball
below the solar plexus
and my arms try to contain this leaping life
he says to me, 'I will always come'
and I reply, 'I will always be waiting.'

THE END

Acknowledgements

MY WARMEST THANKS TO:

Sarojini Vittachi: as always, my first reader and my constant support

Titus (aka Gerard) Pinto: our rock and our strength in the Nilgiris

Bops and Deejay: for allowing us to experience the joys of the magical cottage

Sajai Jose: my as-yet-unmet critic

Karthika V.K. and Udayan Mitra: for loving Joshua sight unseen

Pradipta Sarkar: belatedly, for the miracle she wrought with my first book of poetry

Edgar de Mello: for building our new home and Paulette De Mello: for taking me to the movies every Sunday, from afar

And to Sunil and Christophe: for being there.

About the Author

Tanya Mendonsa is a poet and a painter. She graduated in English from Calcutta, and later moved to Paris to paint, major in French literature at the Sorbonne and run a chaotic language school. After twenty years in Europe, she returned to live in India, in Bangalore, with the abstract painter Antonio E. Costa. They then moved to Goa and now live in the Nilgiri Hills in South India with their dogs.

Tanya has exhibited her paintings widely, but her focus is on her writing. In her poems, she draws deeply from a poetic tradition of the wonders of the natural world, which illuminate her books of poetry, *The Dreaming House* and *All the Answer I Shall Ever Get* (both published by HarperCollins). *The Fisher of Perch* (Paper Project, Chennai) and *Infinite Memories* (Ed. Signum, Paris) were published in 2017. Her poems have been anthologized in the US and in India. *The Book of Joshua* is her first work of non-fiction.

Tanya can be reached at a_ecosta@yahoo.com.